IT Security Governance Guidebook with Security Program Metrics on CD-ROM

IT Security Governance Guidebook with Security Program Metrics on CD-ROM

FRED COHEN

Auerbach Publications
Taylor & Francis Group
Boca Raton New York

Auerbach Publications is an imprint of the
Taylor & Francis Group, an informa business

Supplementary Resources Disclaimer

Additional resources were previously made available for this title on CD. However, as CD has become a less accessible format, all resources have been moved to a more convenient online download option.

You can find these resources available here: https://www.routledge.com/9780849384356

Please note: Where this title mentions the associated disc, please use the downloadable resources instead.

Auerbach Publications
Taylor & Francis Group
6000 Broken Sound Parkway NW, Suite 300
Boca Raton, FL 33487-2742

© 2007 by Fred Cohen
Auerbach is an imprint of Taylor & Francis Group, an Informa business

No claim to original U.S. Government works
Printed in the United States of America on acid-free paper
10 9 8 7 6 5 4 3 2 1

International Standard Book Number-10: 0-8493-8435-4 (Hardcover)
International Standard Book Number-13: 978-0-8493-8435-6 (Hardcover)

Library of Congress Cataloging-in-Publication Data

Cohen, Fred.
   IT security governance guidebook with security program metrics / Fred Cohen.
      p. cm. -- (Cisco toolkit ; 1)
   Includes bibliographical references and index.
   ISBN 0-8493-8435-4 (alk. paper)
      1. Computer networks--Security measures. 2. Computers--Access control. 3. Confidential business information--Security measures--Data processing. 4. Corporate governance. 5. Software measurement. I. Title.

TK5105.59.C57918 2006
005.8--dc22   2006048965

Visit the Taylor & Francis Web site at
http://www.taylorandfrancis.com

and the Auerbach Web site at
http://www.auerbach-publications.com

Table of Contents

The Governance Guidebook

Executive Summary

The *CISO Toolkit* is a collection of books and software for the chief information security officer (CISO) of a substantial enterprise. The *Governance Guidebook* describes the basic structure of information protection and protection programs in enterprises. It is designed to provide clear and concise explanations of key issues in information protection with pictures that allow the material to be presented, referenced, and understood.

This guidebook starts with the structure of information protection at a very high level and rapid pace, but the graphics provide a lot more detail than the explanations. The goal is to provide a rapid-fire overview of material that the typical CISO already understands, along with simple ways it can be explained at a high level to others.

The second part of this guidebook is a drill-down into the details of the items covered in the overview. The goal of the drill-down is to provide at least one level of additional detail for everything explained in the structural guide. In many cases, two levels of detail are provided. This acts as a reference for the CISO so that, when reviewing any particular issue, a more comprehensive set of details relating to that issue can be explored, starting with the coverage provided and extended or curtailed as appropriate to the task at hand.

It has proven most useful for readers to read the structural overview first, then review all of the drill-down sections, and then return for a reread of the structural section. Most readers find the first section complex on the first reading and have many questions, but after the second reading, the reference value of the first section becomes far greater, and it acts as a handy way to remind them of things and explain the structural aspects to others, with drill-down only where needed for the particular use.

To summarize:

1. Read the structural part but don't worry about the lack of initial detail.
2. Read the drill-down for more detailed explanations.

3. Reread the structural part for clarity.
4. Use the structural part to explain top-level issues to others.
5. Use the drill-down for more in-depth review and reference as needed.

About This Material

You may notice that this material contains some complex pictures and diagrams. Perhaps they seem too complex and busy at first. People sometimes ask me during presentations why I have such complex and busy slides. My answer is simple. Because I am a busy guy, and my job is complex. They may try to explain to me that the purpose of the slides is to simplify and provide a way of thinking about the issues. I explain to them that these slides are not for teaching novices about the subject matter; they are for helping experts make sure they don't miss things, and to make sure that the relationships at two or three levels of depth are clear. They tell me that nobody will want to read these complex pictures and explanations. I explain to them that when looking at pictures of all the bones in the human body in an anatomy book, or a payables sheet with aging, or a circuit diagram of a microprocessor or mother board, there are more items shown in less space than in any of my diagrams. Eventually, some of them get it. This book is a blueprint of information protection for a large complex enterprise. Just as the wiring diagram for a building is complicated because there are a lot of wires doing a lot of things, the blueprint of information protection for a global enterprise is complicated because there is a lot to it.

Chapter 1

The Structure of Information Protection

Security governance is similar in many ways to other corporate governance. It has the same basic principles and operates within the same basic structures, but it has significantly unique content and requires individuals with specific skills and influence in order to be effective.

1.1 A Comprehensive Information Protection Program

The comprehensive information protection program eventually starts with how the business works and ends with assuring proper protection of content and its business utility. Oversight defines duties to protect; risk management turns these duties into decisions about risk acceptance, transfer, avoidance, and mitigation, and identifies what to protect. Executive security management then figures out how to protect and use power and influence over organizations to gain control.

Organizational issues and business processes drive control architecture and interact with technical security architecture to affect the protection processes. These processes ultimately control protective mechanisms that interact directly with content and its business utility to assure that risk is adequately mitigated to suit the needs of the organization.

1.1.1 The Architectural Model

The security architecture diagram depicts the elements of organizational security architecture and how they interact with each other. The presentation here is slanted toward a corporate view in terms of the usage, but essentially all elements are always present.

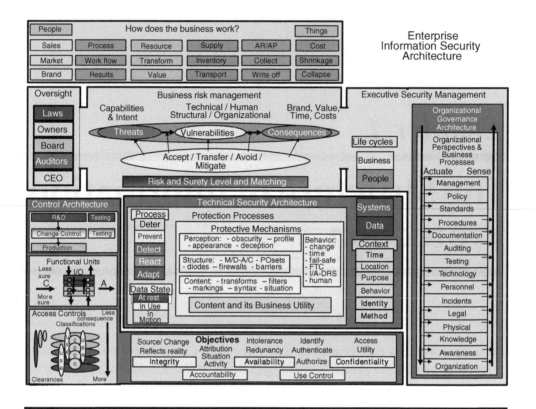

At the top is the notion of how the "business" works. At a detailed level this may be codified in terms of process diagrams and associated details such as timeliness requirements, consequences of failures of different sorts, internal and external interdependencies, and so forth. At a higher level it is divided into different common functions such as sales, marketing, and brand — or resources that get transformed and produce value. These comprise the basic functions of the organization and the foundation for analysis of the value and import of its function or utility.

Oversight comes from laws, owners, the board of directors or similar entity, auditors, and the chief executive officer. It produces a set of duties to protect, which include legal and regulatory duties, contractual duties, and self-imposed duties. It is also tasked with the responsibility for making certain that the duties imposed are carried out.

The business risk-management function seeks to transform the duties to protect into a set of identified things to protect and surety levels associated with that protection, matched to the risks associated with failures and taking into account the complex nature of these issues. As a side effect of this process, understanding of risks in the form of threats, vulnerabilities, and consequences; event sequences that could induce potentially serious negative consequences; interdependencies and risk aggregation issues; decisions about risk acceptance, avoidance, transfer, and mitigation; and notions of acceptable residual risk are provided to enterprise security management for their use and to oversight for their approval.

Enterprise security management transforms the duty to protect, what to protect, and the other outcomes of oversight and risk management process into the actions taken by the organization to implement protection through the use of power and influence. Although the Chief Information Security Officer (CISO) or other responsible parties tasked with these issues typically have little budget, their position and standing provide them with the necessary influence to get the job done if they know how to apply that influence effectively. Specifically, they have positional power that grants them access to information required to get feedback from the organizational processes they influence and adequate influence to adapt those processes to meet the needs of the organization. If these conditions are not met, then the program will fail and the enterprise will suffer the consequences.

The enterprise operates protection through the creation, operation, and adaptation of a control architecture. The control architecture includes structural mechanisms that obtain security objectives through access control; functional units; mechanisms that use identification, authentication, and authorization to provide for use; change control; and other nonarchitectural mechanisms for specific situational reactions.

The technical security architecture implements technical controls by defining protection processes in the form of defensive processes associated with data states and contexts over life cycles of systems and data, and managing them through work-flow controls so as to direct the behaviors of protective mechanisms. Those protective mechanisms come in the form of perception, structure, content, and behavior controls that directly contact the content and assure its ongoing business utility.

In summary, content and business utility are protected by mechanisms, processes, and architectures that are structured through the control architecture and managed via influence on organizational elements by the CISO. The CISO acts to meet the duties to protect by determining how to protect the things that need to be protected and controlling the organization so as to affect those protections. The risk management process and feedback mechanisms guide the CISO and act as the means by which oversight is accomplished with the ultimate objective of assuring that business processes are not interfered with in ways that cause serious negative consequences. The CISO reports to top management, and oversight individuals and groups that have ultimate authority over and responsibility for the business. The effective CISO provides the oversight function with adequate, accurate information to make reasonable and prudent decisions, and carries out those decisions once they are made.

1.1.2 Risk Management

The risk management program tracks threats, vulnerabilities, and consequences in order to determine risk levels and decide which risks to accept, transfer, avoid, and mitigate.

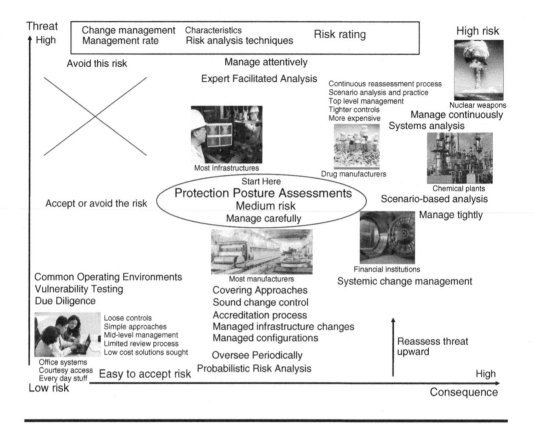

This risk management picture shows risk management processes in the context of threat and consequence levels. Threats increase along the vertical axis and consequences increase along the horizontal axis. When there are low consequences and high threats, the cost of protection, and typically the value of operating the system safely, are not justified. The risk should be avoided. As threats get to the medium level, the risk should either be accepted or avoided because it is not worth mitigating at that consequence level. Transfer is problematic, but it may be achievable. If consequences are considered high and threats are considered low, the threat or consequences assessment should be revisited and an assumption made that threats are likely higher than previously identified. This chart also maps out management process rates, suitable risk assessment processes, change management requirements, risk rating, and other characteristics. Certain business and process types are typically associated with certain threat and consequence levels. For most businesses, the risk management process starts at the center and moves out.

The organizational mapping shows how integrated risk management processes from the comprehensive approach fit into the organizational hierarchy of an enterprise. Top management has responsibility for deterrence, high-level risk management decisions, business life cycles, and high-level organizational issues. As the level of detail increases and the specific factors have to be assessed on a system-by-system basis, project management, implementation

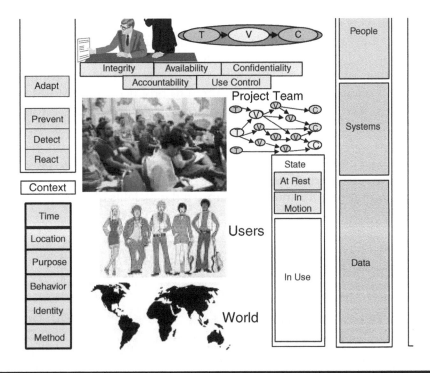

teams, and ultimately users end up bearing the brunt of the effort. They also observe the effects of the protection program and its failures more directly.

Users, for example, have to deal with contextual issues such as when and where they can do what. Systems associated with high valued content and function have to deal with these contextual issues for each user taking each action. Users tend to deal with data life cycles and information at rest, in use, and in transit, and are subject to organizational effects, mandates, and awareness programs as their predominant mode of interaction with the security system. This diagram also expresses the control and feedback associated with different levels of operation in the protection process. For example, project teams tend to use systems and influence technologies, and get feedback from personnel and technology issues associated with the systems they implement.

1.1.3 How the Business Works

In order to be a useful part of a business, information protection has to meaningfully address business issues. Because the function of information and information technology in a business is to help the business function, it is necessary to understand and describe how the business works in order to be able to put and keep information technology and information protection in their proper context. A simplified view of these issues is used in information protection.

Different sorts of businesses work in different ways. They all have people and things; they all have some sort of marketing and sales function that ties to reputation and good will, often codified in the term brand. Businesses have processes that involve work flows to produce results. Most businesses take some sort of resources and transform them to produce value. Most businesses use supplies, have inventory, and transport goods or services through some media. Businesses have accounts receivable and payable, a collection and payment process, and a write-off process that form the basis for accounting. Information technology is an excellent example of a service based on an infrastructure provided to users. Businesses also have cost and shrinkage associated with inventory and can collapse if the weights of costs and shrinkage are too high.

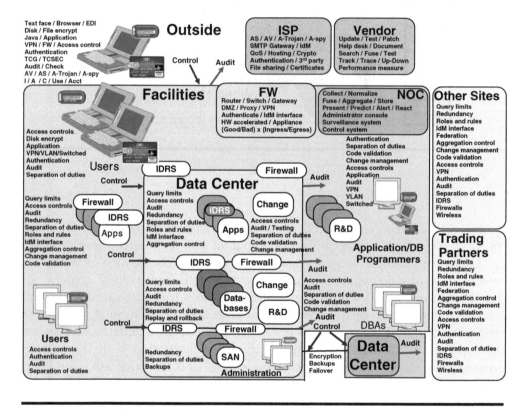

Table 1.1

People	How does the business work?					Things
Sales	Process	Resource	Supply	AR/AP	Infrastruc.	Cost
Market	Work flow	Transform	Inventory	Collect	Services	Shrink
Brand	Results	Value	Transport	Write off	Users	Collapse

Although this is obviously a simplification of businesses and how they operate, it can be used to form the basis for understanding businesses in terms that allow the value and import of different business functions and processes to be clarified. From a standpoint of information protection, this is the key understanding necessary to make sense of business processes as they interact with information technology. In effect, process descriptions and diagrams can be formed to indicate how a business works, and the interactions with information technology can be mapped to understand how protection failures can induce business consequences.

1.1.4 How Information Technology Protection Works

Information technology provides support for these business functions, and to the extent these business functions become dependent on that technology, there are consequences associated with failures in that technology. Failures typically involve loss of integrity, availability, confidentiality, use control, or accountability.

The technology illustration gives an overview of protection mechanisms in an enterprise application architecture. Users with different systems and protection capabilities interact with applications either locally or remotely. They interact with infrastructure and application elements within facilities perimeters. Within these facilities, there are typically physical and logical zones, often including a data center for high-valued information assets and links to other data centers for resiliency and access to additional capabilities. Control and audit paths exist throughout. Internal users operate applications for business functions. Application programmers and database administrators do research and development and use change control mechanisms to alter applications, databases, and storage area networks, resulting in interfaces, analytical processes, and storage and retrieval associated with applications. Many technologies are associated with information protection throughout this process. The selection and implementation of protection technologies is a major facet of the risk mitigation process associated with these systems. Without these protection technologies, these business functions would be subject to a wide range of attacks and failures that would reduce their business value to the

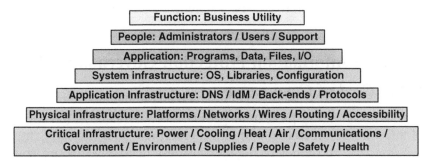

point where they would have little or no real utility because the cost of failures would outweigh the benefits of use. Optimizing protection concurrently optimizes utility of the business applications and systems.

1.1.5 Interdependencies

The interdependency picture shows how business utility depends on complex chains of interdependent information technologies and supporting infrastructures. In order for information technology to operate, all of the dependencies must operate to the level required to service the business function. The technology picture interdependencies associated with technology but ignores the underlying infrastructures that are required for these functions to operate. In using the interdependency viewpoint, the CISO makes many of the implicit assumptions explicit, leading to more detailed consideration and analysis.

The enterprise cannot control all of its dependencies, but it can use redundancy and diversification efforts to reduce the criticality of any individual dependency and thus reduce the aggregation of risks associated with individual components. For example, internationalization reduces the dependency on government stability, and physically diverse locations for data centers eliminates common mode failures associated with dependencies on other critical infrastructure elements.

1.1.6 But How Much Is Enough? The Duty to Protect

A fundamental question that every CISO must answer is how much is enough. Do I need three redundant data centers? Do I need to diversify my dependency on operating systems? Do I need protection at every layer in the technology picture? Do I need to have all of those protective measures? The answers to these questions come from a combination of the duty to protect and risk management decisions. Duty to protect comes from legal and regulatory mandates, contractual obligations, fiduciary duties to shareholders to retain and grow their value, and self-imposed policies. High-level decision-makers reach business decisions that can end their career if they take too much risk and calamity comes, and on the other hand it can end their career if they spend too much mitigating risk and calamity never comes.

1.2 What Is Information Protection Governance All About?

1.2.1 The Goal of Governance

The goal of information protection governance (hereafter governance) is to control information protection within the enterprise so as to make the overall program effective and efficient for the business needs. Needs are commonly defined by top management as including but not limited to:

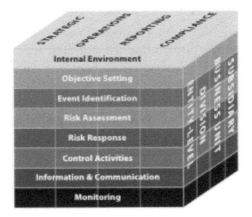

- Meet due diligence requirements to assure that adequate care has been taken to protect shareholder value. Meet the level of care taken in comparable organizations, and be reasonable and prudent for the situation at hand.
- Meet regulatory requirements associated with laws such as the Sarbanes–Oxley (SOX). The COSO Cube is an example of a governance structure associated with risk management mandated by regulators for SOX compliance.
- Meet health information and other privacy-related regulations in their different forms around the world.
- Meet industry-specific requirements such as food and drug production and tracking controls, financial institution controls, and jurisdictional requirements, such as privacy mandates and prohibitions against encryption, of different countries.
- Meet contractual requirements such as those associated with regulatory mandated contracts for sharing of information, contract language associated with confidentiality and intellectual property, performance goals, and service level agreements.
- Fulfill business needs for integrity, availability, confidentiality, use control, and accountability for actions, and of course assure ongoing utility of information and systems even in the presence of malicious attacks that are widely present in the environment today.
- Address physical factors and disaster scenarios such as weather, earth movement, tsunamis, explosions, and other threats to business continuity.
- React effectively to changes in the business environment, competitive threats, and changing worker profiles.
- Meet profit and loss objectives, control costs, and understand and demonstrate what the enterprise is getting for its money.

Governance creates the internal business conditions that allow these needs to be met and balanced through effective control of key components of business and information operations.

1.2.2 What Are the Aspects of Governance?

Governance is the process by which government operates. This is comprised of structures, rules, power and influence, funding mechanisms, enforcement mechanisms, and appeals processes. Ultimately, in order for the information protection function to be effective, it must fit into the governance structures of the enterprise. The ultimate goal of information security governance is to implement an effective, efficient, and comprehensive information protection program within the context of the enterprise.

1.2.2.1 Structures

The structure of the government and its relationship to the governed are fundamental elements of governance. This starts with structural elements:

- Hierarchical structures are quite common. They are used to leverage increasing numbers of people with decreasing power and influence, lower pay rates, increasing specialization and specialized expertise, fewer privileges, and more differentiated tasks at lower levels of the hierarchy where they perform more tactical and less strategic tasks. Dictatorships, military groups, and many companies use hierarchy. Knowledge is controlled and propaganda or similar cultural control mechanisms are used to facilitate power and influence over large numbers of people.
- Networked organizations are structured with sets of key participants who take on leadership roles in select areas, and many other participants who work independently but form a consensus that moves the group forward. Knowledge is widely available to anyone who wishes to seek it, and strategy and tactics are developed by consensus. Pay and responsibility tend to be based on performance levels and infrastructure ownership. These organizations are often called "organic" in the way they operate, but most of them in fact have elite classes that communicate independently in cliques and use the network to their advantage by limiting access to information or selectively feeding information to the group as fits their desires. Sometimes, juntas form in these sorts of groups, and these groups sometimes turn into hierarchies as size increases.
- Matrix organizations typically involve sets of leaders associated with different aspects of the functional need. There may be financial leaders, functional leaders, project leaders, line of business leaders, and so forth. Power is distributed, and strategy and tactics are shared across groups that form for tasks. Matrix organizations without central leadership or strong management communications tend to produce schizophrenic overall behaviors as individuals are forced to serve multiple masters with differing and often contradictory demands.
- Hub and spoke structures are somewhat more rare and tend to be limited in size because of the critical role of the central leader. The central leader tends to be charismatic in nature for medium-sized organizations and may be a small business owner for smaller organizations. Power and finance

are centralized, and strategy and tactics are only shared as needed, typically all directed toward fulfilling the vision of the leader.

■ Mixed structures, like most governments, large organizations, and businesses if viewed in detail, tend to be composites of these structures. For example, the U.S. government is a networked infrastructure at the topmost level with many hierarchies, hub and spoke, and matrix management structures at lower levels. The sharing of power is typically achieved by these mixed structures, and all powerful individuals at any level of the organization tend to build the structure they are most familiar with or they think is most appropriate to the needs of their business function.

Each of these structures has particular processes that work more and less efficiently within them, they have advantages and disadvantages, and they are all suitable to different situations. The structure of the enterprise and its components necessarily dictates the structure of the overall information protection program and the manner in which those tasked with governing the process are able to influence the protection posture, measure results, fund the effort, and deal with objections.

1.2.2.2   What Are the Rules?

The CISO has responsibility for creating and following formal and informal, written and unwritten rules. Formal rules are easier to understand and define. They come from a variety of sources and have varying punishments associated with failures to follow them.

Policies are the codification of internal rules in documented form. But real rules of how companies work are rarely codifiable in those terms. Policies are used to derive control standards that codify more detailed situations, change more often, and have shorter approval processes at more local levels. Control standards constrain procedures that codify sequences of specific actions for specific circumstances. They change even more often, are more locally controlled, and take less time to change. For example, a policy that indicates audit information to be read-only may produce a control standard mandating append-only files for systems with access controls. This leads to a procedure to set protection bits in a mainframe. These include, produce, and require documentation that forms a contemporaneous record of the rules and how well they are followed.

Official rules tend to pass through organizational structures. For example, in a hierarchy, orders come down from above and may not be appealed unless they are thought to be in violation of policies set by top leadership. Even in these cases, the challenger is facing an uphill battle and has the burden of proof. In a matrix environment, different people have responsibilities to fulfill their mandates, and their ability to command effort derives from those mandates. But the individual has to decide how to prioritize the different requests and to understand where their loyalties lie. The rules may be more complex and even contradictory in some circumstances. In the hub systems, the center of the hub is simply in charge. The ability to control these systems is limited by the concentration of power and the limits of cognition, focus of attention, and bandwidth of the leader. Networked organizations are driven by effort more than rules. This makes explicit control far harder to accomplish, leaving control to those who have the ability to build consensus by exerting other sorts of influence.

1.2.2.3   Principles and Standards

The Generally Accepted Information Security Principles (GAISP) standard provides a starting point for understanding the basic principles of effective information security governance. It provides a standards-based approach to understanding the rules that should be in place and, because it is a standard, it can be used to assert diligence. It includes pervasive principles, broad functional principles, and detailed principles. The pervasive principles include:

- **Accountability:** Information security accountability and responsibility must be clearly defined and acknowledged.
- **Awareness:** All parties with a need to know should have access to principles, standards, conventions, or mechanisms for the security of information and information systems and should be informed of applicable threats to the security of information.
- **Ethics:** Information should be used, and the administration of information security should be executed, in an ethical manner.
- **Multidisciplinary:** Security should address the considerations and viewpoints of all interested parties.
- **Proportionality:** Controls should be proportionate to risks.
- **Integration:** Security elements should be coordinated and integrated.
- **Timeliness:** Accountable parties should act in a timely and coordinated manner to prevent or respond to threats and attacks.
- **Assessment:** Risks should be assessed periodically.
- **Equity:** Management must respect the rights and dignity of individuals when setting policy and implementing protection.

The earlier generally accepted system security principles (GASSP) also included:

- **Certification and accreditation:** Information systems and information security professionals should be certified to be technically competent and approved by management for operations.
- **Internal control:** Information security forms the core of an organization's information internal control system.
- **Adversary:** Controls, security strategies, architectures, policies, standards, procedures, and guidelines should be developed and implemented in anticipation of attack from intelligent, rational, and irrational adversaries with harmful intent or harm from negligent or accidental actions.
- **Least privilege:** An individual should be granted enough privilege to accomplish assigned tasks, but no more. This principle should be applied with increased rigor as the potential for damage increases.

- **Separation of duties:** Responsibilities and privileges should be allocated so as to prevent an individual or a small group of collaborating individuals from causing unacceptable harm or loss.
- **Continuity:** The organization's needs for continuity of operations should be anticipated and adequately protected and planned for.
- **Simplicity:** Information security professionals should favor small and simple safeguards over large and complex safeguards.
- **Policy-centered security:** Policies, standards, and procedures should be established to serve as a basis for management planning, control, and evaluation of information security activities.

These principles are also codified in the Organization for Economic Cooperation and Development (OECD) principles that are approved by nations around the globe. Other approaches are also available.

In each of these systems of governance, the information protection program is supposed to use the formal rules and the rule generation and appeals process to create a protection posture suited to the needs of the enterprise. Policies, standards, and processes are put in place to create the environment that fosters appropriate protection. But this is only the start of the overall process.

In addition to written rules of the enterprise, there are many unwritten social rules that play an important part in governance. People have to get along with each other, understand where they fit into the enterprise and where the CISO and those carrying out information protection functions fit. Social processes and influence are involved in clarifying these relationships. This means that, at the enterprise level, the people tasked with information protection must be able to effectively work with both the written and unwritten rules to create the entire information protection program. This is where power and influence come into play, and this is one of the many reasons that the CISO position must be properly placed within the enterprise in order to be effective.

1.2.2.4 Power and Influence

Power and influence have been studied for a long time. The basic principles associated with them are outlined and discussed briefly here.

Power comes in many different forms and is directly applied in order to indirectly produce influence. The key to understanding the role of power and influence from a governance standpoint is that the individual responsible for coordinating overall information protection in an enterprise must ultimately have enough power to influence the enterprise to produce a comprehensive program that works. This calls for a combination of skills and mandates, as well as a capacity to deal with people. Power is also associated with physical capacity, resources, position, information, right to access, right to organize, expertise, personal charisma, and emotion. These play on:

1. Overt use of force, exchanges, rules and procedures, and persuasion
2. Covert uses of control over environment and personal magnetism
3. The threat of force

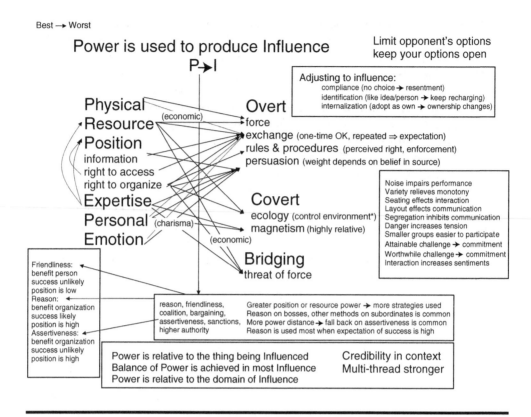

In different organizations and with different people, different methods work. The skilled handlers of power and influence will use these sorts of force while remaining friendly with the vast majority of those they have to work with. The selection of such an individual requires an appropriate management decision and a negotiation process that produces the conditions required for success.

The methodology used to influence different structures is dependent on the specifics of the individual or group trying to create influences and the structure they are trying to influence. For example, a hierarchy is typically moved by moving someone at a high-enough level to effect the desired change. If you go too high in the hierarchy, you may produce the change by virtue of power, but the change may be considered trivial by the person making it, and your credibility may therefore be reduced. If the person is above you in the hierarchy, you cannot change them by force, so you must change them with some other means of influence, perhaps a personal relationship, perhaps the force of logic, perhaps by elements of the environment, and perhaps by influencing others in their peer group to indirectly influence them. The number of situations is large and the potential number of different paths of influence is enormous, but the interested reader can apply these principles and investigate these issues on their own to figure out how to reach and persuade the audience they need to influence.

Many enterprises make the mistake of taking a highly skilled technical person without adequate tools and mandates and expecting that the protection program will grow and prosper under this tutelage. Others make a similar mistake by putting a manager in charge of information protection though he lacks the necessary understanding of the information protection field to make sound judgments about those decisions. Neither is adequate to the task. Some enterprises choose to manage protection by groups, but effective programs have a single individual who is in charge of the overall effort at an enterprise level. That individual creates and operates the groups that produce the results.

The key to success is choosing champions who understand how to influence the organization, understand the technical issues to the point where they cannot be easily fooled, and understand the business to the point where they can help make reasonable and prudent decisions. To be successful, this individual will also need some other things, including but not limited to positional power, adequate resources, and expertise. Specifics should be identified in context and, for those who seek to hire or be posted into such a position, it will be important to identify these matters during the interview process. A decision must also be made about whether to build or buy the champion. Hiring an outsider for such a position may be better if internal expertise is not available or if it will create personnel issues. If inadequate internal expertise is available in an individual, it may be prudent to augment expertise while an internal appointee is further developed.

1.2.2.5   *Funding*

Without adequate funding, security governance will fail. But the problem of determining how much funding is required is far from simple to solve. There is very little publicly available information on security budgets or numbers of incidents and losses, and even if this information were available, what is covered by the protection program and the specifics of the enterprise are critical to gaining useful understanding of these issues. In addition, security costs are often hidden costs, so it is hard to get a good grip on the cost issue even if someone cares to try. Those who have been bold enough to publish this kind of information come to several generally agreed values.

- Systems administration and security, which are inexorably intertwined, account for about 5% of all of the time and expenses involved in using computers. This includes 1 out of every 20 people using computers, and 1 out of 20 dollars spent on hardware, software, maintenance, operations, and management for everyone who deals with information technology in their work.
- Costs of regulatory compliance during periods between the introduction of new regulations and their normalization in the enterprise have been reported in the range of 8% of total IT budgets by large enterprises. In normal operation, these same companies reported 4% of total IT budget for meeting compliance requirements.

- Financial institutions evaluated as having a reasonable, prudent, and effective program relative to common standards such as the GAISP, ISO17799, and this book's evaluation scheme typically spend from 10% to 20% of their IT budget on information protection.
- Physical security is also required for information protection to be effective. The cost of physically secured facilities, depending on the specific security needs, ranges from two to ten times the cost of normal unsecured office space.
- Costs tend to be dominated by operations rather than acquisitions. As a rule of thumb, operating costs per quarter equal acquisition costs for security-related hardware and software if operated for effective protection.

Each enterprise is unique, and these numbers depend on factors ranging from business location to competitive environment. Metrics widely available today are inadequate for providing better information.

But perhaps more important than how much funding is needed is where the money comes from and where it goes. This is largely dictated by organizational structures and responsibilities. Sometimes it is taken out of "hide" (from budgets of) programs and business units throughout the enterprise or gets expressed as a tax or charge-back for services rendered. But the overall protection program clearly involves many different hides, and trying to assess strict values to protection services is problematic. Companies do not normally account for security costs accurately and tend to keep them as hidden costs. When accountants who know something more than their neighbor about a Trojan horse scanner help others run the scanner, this is not accounted for. The training time associated with information security awareness programs is rarely accounted for, and the increased time and effort associated with security-related inconvenience is generally ignored in bookkeeping systems. As a result, it is difficult to really say where the costs of an information protection program come from or go to.

One of the things that CISOs should try to do is get a handle on these costs and try to track them. A simple approach is to get estimates from individuals throughout the enterprise by making a list of the places they likely spend time and effort by asking them to fill in a chart. The chart is then collected for a statistically significant number of individuals per type and analyzed to get an expected cost across the enterprise. A more accurate and more expensive approach is to observe individuals and try to gather enough statistics to give a good indication of the actual costs. In either case, this is typically done as the maturity of the program increases with the objective of trying to optimize the program at a fairly fine-grained level. The chart provided here can be used to carry out such a survey. Additional rows may be needed for your enterprise.

There are some costs that are clearly designated as security-related and accounted for as such. These are usually related to the structure of the program.

Table 1.2 A Sample Hidden Costs Data Collection Sheet

Area of Likely Cost	How Much?
Time to authenticate	
Performance degradation from encryption	
Time spent helping others with security issues	
Time spent reporting or responding to incidents	
Time spent in security awareness training not charged back	
Cost of extra software for security requirements	
Installation, maintenance, and update time for security software	
Time delays in booting up or logging in from security scans, etc.	
Delays while running programs for security-related issues	
Costs of multiple authentications after initial sign-on	
Help desk calls related to lost passwords	
Costs of having to shut down and restart for security reasons	
Time wasted during security-related outages of systems or networks	
Time spent in backups not centrally managed and accounted for	
Time spent in security-related documentation	
Time spent reviewing security-related policies and reading contracts	
Time spent in gaining additional approvals for exceptions	
Cost of delays associated with authentications for external access	
Relationship costs because of security requirements met and unmet	

1.2.2.6 Enforcement Mechanisms

People do not always get and stay with the information protection program as well as they should. Attackers almost never do. Insiders who are abusing systems for their own advantage also tend to not obey all the rules. But even the average worker who wants to do the right thing may have some difficulties always getting it right from a security standpoint. An example of doing the right thing and having the program fail occurs when diligent employees place sensitive information in shred bins. In many installations, these bins are easily opened. When opened by strangers in the area, no challenges are made. The result is a program that provides attackers with ready access to the most sensitive information.

When the program is not followed, there must be an enforcement mechanism that results in detection and reaction to significant protection irregularities before they result in serious negative consequences. Similarly, when a program is followed and the result is worse than if it were not followed, there must be mechanisms in place to detect and adapt to these irregularities before they cause serious negative consequences. These mechanisms ultimately tie into the overall management feedback system because, in addition to any automated technical responses, the management process must also produce appropriate human responses that are consistent with company policies and needs.

Enforcement is produced through the enterprise governance process. It may involve a direct supervisor, the HR department, computer security personnel, the owners of affected systems, law enforcement, private investigators, the legal department, internal committees, and executive management. It might result in anything from a minor change in a detection threshold to a large-scale adaptation of the enterprise protection posture and civil or criminal litigation. Because of the wide range of possibilities, the governance process should produce protection policies, standards, and procedures that intermingle with the HR policies, standards, and procedures to define the enforcement process.

Significant documentation requirements exist for these processes, including documentation that demonstrates that:

- Processes are followed.
- Forensic data is properly treated.
- Legal and regulatory reporting requirements are met.
- Sanctions are properly and consistently applied without discrimination, based on legally restricted bases.
- Other enforcement documentation exists, as dictated by the legal department.

Despite the need to assure a uniform process, there are different processes for individuals of different status, such as employees, contractors, visitors, suppliers, customers, and others. Each has different background, training, awareness, restrictions on, and punishments for violations of terms of use. For customers, this is particularly problematic because a violation of a policy or work rule cannot be summarily dismissed, but it might be a sensitive area that causes loss of business if improperly handled. Misdeeds of contractor employees are the responsibility of the contractor; however, in practice, it is difficult to do the same level of training for contractor employees as for internal employees who, presumably but not uniformly, have more longevity with and dedication to the company.

Similar to the legal system in general, administrative punishments may be defined in terms of the specific violations of policy involved and have to meet a standard of consistency in order to prevent wrongful discharge and discrimination-related legal processes from being successfully invoked.

Many enterprises have made the mistake of treating executives differently from lower-level employees when they violate protection policies, and some have found themselves in situations where they end up covering up serious criminal acts as a result. This is always a mistake. Executives should be treated like any other employees when it comes to violations of laws or policies. In many cases, executives are actually employed by a holding company that may have different work rules, benefits, and so forth. This is problematic as well, and yet it certainly does and must exist in many enterprises.

Enforcement may, of course, have some discretionary aspects to it. For example, a supervisor may determine whether an event warrants action based on the context of the event. An employee who uses a short password on a system in violation of a generic enterprise password policy may be in technical violation of that policy, but if the system only allows short passwords, the employee cannot reasonably be taken to task over it. Many policies allow discretion, and the employee history or relationship with management may dictate different responses to similar incidents. Again, these are governance issues that should be addressed and included in training for all those who have a role that allows such discretion to be exercised. Documentation is also critical for such situations.

At higher levels, enforcement becomes problematic because of power issues. Even though a corporate policy is in place, powerful enough managers or executives may simply disregard the policy for their part of the enterprise. If management does not enforce policy, the policy becomes an even bigger problem because the company may be subject to legal actions for failure to follow their policies when they would not be subject to those actions without those policies. Enforcement at these levels sometimes must be dealt with by top management. The power and influence of the individual tasked with information protection governance must be effective in order to protect the enterprise at this level.

Contractual obligations create other security-related enforcement issues. For example, the inability to effectively control consultants and other off-premise contractors leads to their ability to violate policies, standards, and procedures almost without recourse. In the United States, independent contractor work rules cannot be enforced under the IRS code without turning them into employees and thus granting them undesired legal status, access to benefits, and so forth. There are contractual ways to create proper conditions for these consultants and independent contractors, but they must be specifically attended to in information protection governance in order to get them right and adapt them to changing needs over time. This implies that security governance must interact with the legal department to create the proper conditions for contracts.

Contractual issues also apply to duties to protect information provided under:

- Intellectual property controls, including trade secret, patent, and copyright
- Private information associated with trading partners such as those covered under contracts for services
- Contract terms that may be required with trading partners for one reason or another
- Privacy policies that are announced to the public such as those relating to information collected on Web sites and paper contracts
- Safe harbor agreements such as those associated with European Union (EU) privacy regulation,
- Classification-related contractual requirements, typically associated with government contracts in different jurisdictions
- Health-related information about individuals, like those covered by the Health Information Portability and Accountability Act (HIPAA) agreements required for exchange of data with third parties
- Financial information protected under the Gramm-Leach-Bliley (GLB) act, the Sarbanes-Oxley (SOX) act, and other similar and related regulations requiring contracts associated with information protection

These and other contractual obligations may place nearly arbitrary constraints on select classes of information, and thus it is vital that the enterprise be able to separate information, based on applicable protection requirements (typically called a *classification scheme*) and enforce different rules about information protection with respect to each of these different sorts of information. Typically these approaches include (1) a clearance process so that individuals who have proper characteristics, backgrounds, and training associated with handling of different sorts of information are given clearances to access different categories of information, and (2) need-to-know and need-to-use provisions so that only those individuals working on efforts relevant to the information have access based on their use of that information in their jobs.

1.2.2.7   Appeals Processes and Disputes

Ultimately, disputes happen and people do not like decisions that are made. This can end up in one of three ways: It can lead to a legal process that extends beyond the border of the enterprise, it can lead to an acceptance of the decision, or it can lead to an internal adjudication process. Acceptance is preferred, but internal process is necessary to reduce the number of external processes.

The internal appeals and dispute resolution process is a critical part of protection governance. It should be built into policies, typically through provisions for policy override by someone at an appropriate level of management. Standards and procedures should codify the policies regarding appeals and disputes so that they are handled in a uniform manner that is consistent with HR standards and processes as well as regulatory or contractual requirements. The appeals process and each instance of its use should be documented.

This process is greatly complicated in cases where subcontractors are involved, and inadequate contractual provisions are provided. This is one of the reasons that effective governance must integrate with the legal department in creating standard terms and conditions related to all external contracts. Appeals processes for contractors are typically nonexistent in nongovernment contracts, and the lack of such processes tends to lead contractors to violate policies that interfere with getting their job done. For example, if internal requirements indicate the need to encrypt all e-mail but the contractor has an internal-only e-mail system that runs over secured infrastructure and affords equivalent protection without encryption, they may ignore enterprise policies for internal communications and risk being dismissed. If they could notify the enterprise of the condition and ask permission, they would not have to ignore policy and might get the exception.

Disputes at higher levels tend to be settled by negotiation processes. Some of these are subtle and indirect, whereas others are far more formal, in some cases leading to litigation. A typical example is worker monitoring where disagreements between unions and management have led to several legal and arbitration cases. In most such cases, proper governance can dramatically reduce the number, cost, and complexity of these disputes.

In some cases, disputes have to be settled by external bodies. For example, in resolving matters associated with clearances an external body is often involved for higher-level clearance issues associated with government contracts. Other legal processes may get involved as well, sometimes leading to arbitration, settlement negotiations, and civil or criminal cases. It is almost always better to settle disputes internally; however, sometimes there is no choice.

1.2.3 *The Overall Control System*

Together, the elements of governance described here produce and implement a control system that is at the heart of what information protection governance is about. The control system typically involves a decision-making body that is guided by an individual who is tasked with information security governance. The decision-making body depends on inputs it gets from external sources, from the individual tasked with governance, and from enterprisewide feedback mechanisms. It exerts influence through the full diversity of actions available through the powers vested in it, with the enterprise lead ultimately using those powers to influence the enterprise to be properly protected.

Most complex systems are hard to control. As a result, many different viewpoints exist on how this control works, and it works differently in different enterprises. Some enterprise chief information security officers (CISOs) assert that they control the protection program by directly controlling budget, having approval processes in place, and otherwise placing observation and actuation points throughout the enterprise. Others assert that control is grown by providing moral guidance and setting minimum standards of behavior that create an environment in which protection-supportive behaviors become the social norm. Still others create and operate collaborations with many others throughout the enterprise and become an advisory body with high-level influence, never forcing any issue at all. Most CISOs find mixes of these strategies for different situations.

These approaches and many others are all valid, as long as they are effective at meeting the information protection governance requirements of the enterprise. This brings us to the fundamentals of control. In order for a control system to be effective, it must have three things:

- Adequate numbers and placement of accurate sensors to measure meaningful observables and report them
- Adequate numbers and placements of effective actuators to induce desired system behaviors
- An analytical system that uses sensor and state information to produce actions that operate the enterprise within the desired control envelope

Most enterprise information protection control systems have limited sensors and actuators and rely on individuals with special skills to compensate for all

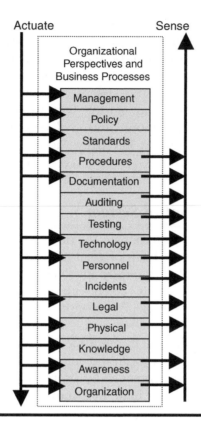

of the other failings in the system on a case-by-case basis. This often produces failed governance programs, negative audit reports, dramatic failures and mitigations, unpleasant security-related surprises, costly regulatory-forced changes, and other similar substantial negative consequences.

1.3 Fitting Protection into Business Structures

Effective information protection programs are structured for the businesses they serve because this tends to minimize friction and result in more effective control. Most businesses are either oriented toward a market segment with centralized top management and a hierarchy, or are a family of companies with a small central management group and independent internal management at each of the operating entities. Mixes exist where large divisions act more independently than smaller ones with some business functions, like corporate communications, payroll, accounting, human resources (HR), and information services organized as central service organizations. Facilities may have both distributed and centralized elements, and many enterprises divide along national boundaries for legal and regulatory compliance reasons.

1.3.1 Fitting In

Regardless of the overall corporate structure, information protection has to fit into it, and as a rule of thumb, information protection should not be significantly different from other existing corporate-wide functions. If a brand new model is used for information protection, it will likely cause friction because integration with the rest of the enterprise will be unnecessarily complicated. But though integration of information protection into overall business operation is critical to success, the many touch points and the need to integrate across a wide breadth of functions, business units, and levels makes it unique in many ways.

The most common approach is to treat information protection in a manner similar to other crosscutting business functions, like finance and accounting (F&A), HR, or corporate communications. For the purposes of discussion and presentation, this analogy may help to clarify this issue. The CISOs might compare information protection function and structure with HR, F&A, or other crosscutting functions within their own enterprise. Look at the information protection issues and identify all of the touch points within the enterprise. Consider risk management, business functions, organizational issues, life cycles, attack and defense processes, contexts, data states, and protection objectives, and how each of these interacts with the enterprise. Seen through this lens, the enterprise governance picture for information protection will be clarified.

1.3.2 The Theory of Groups

The depth and diversity of the information protection function and the need for crosscutting implementation and involvement dictates the need for groups of people to get involved in making decisions and carrying them out. The theory of groups says, in simplest form, that effective groups have enough people with top quality skills and knowledge in relevant areas to cover the issues of import to the purpose of the group, and as few excess people as feasible. Hence:

- The reason for coverage is so that important things are not missed.
- The reason for high quality experts is to assure that the best information is brought to the group.
- The reason for limiting redundancy is that it is inefficient. It wastes time and effort of experts. Where experts disagree, they tend to waste the time of the rest of the group over relatively minor differences.
- Adequate redundancy is important to assure that there aren't significant holes, but excessive overlap is not desirable.

Another common understanding about the group process is that it goes through three phases: (1) storming, in which the members have significant friction as they meet each other and adapt to the new context; (2) norming, in which the group members normalize their behaviors to each other by determining what will and will not work in the group context; and (3) performing, in which the group gets work done efficiently with a minimum of friction. The goal is to reach a performing stage quickly and retain it for most of the effort.

A third important group-related issue is that as groups age, they become stable in their configuration and tend to innovate less. They may form cliques or become a clique as a whole. This tends to lead to similar thought patterns and roles played by individuals that limit their overall utility in the group. The group becomes static and stale, and subject to group think, in which even things that would appear obviously foolish to an outsider are considered reasonable by the group because of their context with each other. To avoid this situation, it is necessary to shake up such groups periodically. This costs some short-term performance but improves long-term performance.

These theories should be applied in governance of the information protection function within the enterprise. To this end:

- Optimize group performance by combining the right set of experts from the different relevant areas without excessive redundancy.
- Operate groups on a regular basis and keep them stable over time.
- Force a reasonable level of turnover or other dynamics to stay fresh and avoid group think.

1.3.3 What Groups Are Needed

Many different groups are involved in information protection functions within an enterprise, and governance is needed to deal with these groups and keep them running properly. For each IT project, there is an information protection element involved, and the individual with that function for that group has to have the information and understanding necessary to interface between enterprise and project protection functions. Once projects enter into processes that turn them into enterprise business functions, they have to join the fold of enterprise information protection, including all of the facets discussed in the comprehensive information protection approach. That approach involves fifteen organizational and business perspectives, four types of life cycles, five elements of the attack and defense process, five different sorts of objectives, six different contextual elements, the risk management framework, and how the business works. In large enterprises there are 25 or so enterprisewide groups involved in this process and a central group that may be mirrored in business units that is responsible for managing this overall process. Together with leaders of these groups and an enterprise-level leadership role integrated with top management, they form the institutions that are governance. Typical groups include:

- Top-level and business unit governance boards
- Policy, standards, and procedures group, and review board
- HR and Legal groups, and review boards
- Risk management group and review board

Top Executives Board of Directors									
CISO Functions and Management									
Policy Standards Procedures	HR Legal	Risk	Testing and Change Control	Technical safeguards physical / information	Incidents	Auditing	Knowledge Awareness	Document	

- Protection testing and change control group and review board
- Informational and physical safeguards groups and review boards
- Incident handling and business continuity group and review board
- Protection audit group and review board
- Awareness and knowledge group, and review board
- Internal and external review, and advisory boards
- Zoning boards, security architecture groups, and review boards
- Project-specific groups for special efforts

Operating this set of groups consumes most of the time and effort of the CISO.

1.4   Who Is in Charge and Who Does This Person Work for?

We will call the individual responsible for operating the enterprise information protection function the chief information security officer (CISO).

1.4.1 The CISO

The CISO has indirect influence over a large number of people and direct control over a smaller team. The CISO typically has a staff of about ten direct reports who control or influence others throughout the enterprise through their leadership in various groups and review boards.

1.4.2 The CISO's Team

The 10 CISO staff members and their qualifications should typically include:

- **Staff assistant:** A well seasoned enterprise employee who knows how enterprise administrative processes and systems work, has strong technical and communications skills, and knows many other workers. Strong project management and documentation skills are a must.
- **Policy, standards, and procedures lead:** These individuals should have some legal training or background and understanding of technical issues

in information protection and business systems. They should be detail oriented, have strong writing and language skills, be willing and able to deal with legalese, and have strong library skills. They often use outside consultants to develop and update policies.

■ **Legal, investigation, and risk management team lead:** These functions are often combined because of synergistic skill sets and the need for close coordination of these issues. Typically they have at least ten years in the enterprise, strong analytical, actuarial, and mathematical skills, and book-keeping and investigative backgrounds. Retired law enforcement personnel with additional skills and degrees are often used. Many companies split the position, using a CFO-owned individual for the risk management and a retired law enforcement person for the legal and investigative lead.

■ **Protection testing and change control lead:** Expertise in quality control and quality assurance (QC/QA) and testing is a must. So is technical expertise in a wide range of systems, hardware, software, and operating environments. A master's degree with a focus on information security or systems testing and evaluation is a help. At least ten years of experience in a technical setting is required. Special education and training from outside experts is often necessary.

■ **Technical computer security lead:** Requirements include at least ten years of computer security experience with increasing technical responsibility leading to technical team leadership in large-scale complex projects, strong project management and technical skills across a broad spectrum of system and network types, advanced training or a masters degree in a computer-related area, and the ability to work well with others in groups.

■ **Physical security lead:** Typically, the physical security program is independent of but linked to the information security program. The lead from the physical security team acts as a liaison to the CISO team for physical security issues. If physical security is handled by facilities managers at each facility, a physical security lead within the CISO office is required to coordinate physical security for IT facilities. This individual usually likes to travel, has 20 years of law enforcement background, perhaps some construction and physical sciences background, and has and continues to go through specialized training in information security.

■ **Incident handling and business continuity planning lead:** These leads are responsible for IT-related business continuity planning and disaster recovery, and real-time technical attack and defense — the detect and react processes. They need to understand enterprise business applications and critical interdependencies to design real-time decisions, but they also need strategic understanding and excellent communication and coordination skills to address business continuity. Typically, they are long-term employees with at least 20 years of experience including project management. They need strong vendor management skills and manage external consultants when skills are not internally available.

■ **Audit lead:** Typically this individual is a member of IT audit that has become the team leader after more than ten years of experience because of demonstrated team leadership. The audit lead is typically a representative of the audit team rather than the top technical person.

- **Awareness and knowledge lead:** Necessary requirements include experience in corporate training and awareness programs, all the better if the experience is in security-related areas. This position may be filled by a consultant with a history in information security training and awareness, but should be replaced by a staff training and awareness specialist once the program is fully operational with outside assistance a few weeks per quarter.
- **Personnel and operations security lead:** The ideal candidate has 10 years of counterintelligence experience, work experience leading teams that do background investigations, and sound understanding of technical and human vulnerabilities leading to system and project compromise. This individual is sometimes found in the physical security team.

This grouping is an example but is not prescriptive. Background, expertise, and knowledge for these functions tend to be found together in individuals, but other groupings are reasonable, depending on the specific individuals involved and the amount of work involved in each area.

1.4.3 The Structure of the Groups

These individuals head up teams of different sizes depending on the need for people in each of these areas and the existing population within existing business structures. In smaller enterprises or enterprises with less of an information technology emphasis, more functions may be combined into fewer positions, but care is needed to assure that enough resources and expertise are available to meet the need. If the group gets too small or has inadequate expertise it will fail. For example:

- Many companies have a centralized group for firewall implementation and operation. Such a group is usually under the control of the technical safeguards lead and tight coordination with the incident handling team.
- If the firewall team is within the networking group at the enterprise level, it is moved to a CISO function or retained within networking with matrix management to assure proper overall operation and coordination.
- A telecommunications department that handles their own firewalls might exist within a business unit. This group may be integrated with the CISO organization or kept within the business unit. Coordination with the CISO team can occur at the management and technical level. Reporting structures are then designed to provide information and access to the CISO team to fulfill enterprise needs without disrupting controls.
- A new acquisition might have a firewall team within its CIO office as part of a computer security team. For the transition, a firewall will usually be put between the new acquisition and the rest of the enterprise to limit damage. The firewall lead in the new acquisition will have touch points with the CISO team that change to meet the situation specifics. As the new business unit is integrated, structuring changes to meet enterprise needs.

These examples reflect the overall approach of having security functions integrate with business structures. The interconnectivity and interdependencies associated with security-related systems drive the need to coordinate overall security efforts. Integration across the enterprise ends up being a complex myriad of different arrangements that provide necessary function, coordination, and control. Some amount of restructuring may be used to reduce complexity, but the CISO rarely ends up in direct control over much of the security function. Rather, control and influence are indirect, and a cooperative environment comes into existence. Failures in control are handled in a political process. Inadequate CISO power and influence lead to control failures and the enterprise suffers. If a necessary function does not exist within a portion of the enterprise, the CISO must find a way to get the function in place by directly creating and controlling it, by influencing the business unit to put the function in place, by brokering a deal with another business unit to provide that function, or by other creative means.

1.4.4 Meetings and Groups the CISO Chairs or Operates

The following table gives a roll-up of a meeting schedule guide for these groups. If business units have representatives in these groups, one person per business unit per group should be added to each group for the enterprisewide version.

Scheduled group meeting times account for more than 600 h per year of CISO time. Add in preparation and analysis time, the political and budgeting processes, keeping abreast of current events and keeping the CISO's knowledge level high, strategic planning, emergency involvements, and all of the as-needed activities. This constitutes most of the full-time CISO's schedule.

1.4.5 Should the CISO Work for the CIO or Others?

In many enterprises, the CISO works for the CIO, and in some cases for the CFO or others, but these lines of authority are problematic. The broad range of issues involved in the CISO's job leads to high-level interaction with members of the top management team and their staff. CISO decisions are clearly beyond the scope of the typical CIO or CFO function. Placing the CISOs at a lower organizational level is problematic for their interaction with the rest of the management team.

The most critical reasons that the CISO must be independent stem from (1) the need for the CISO to independently report on security-related matters to the CEO and board of directors, and (2) the requirement for adequate influence and access to information to meet the enterprise duty to protect at the enterprise level. Top-level communication is legally mandated and cannot be intermediated without putting top management and the enterprise at peril. Fulfilling the duty to protect requires adequate influence and information, and the skill to use them effectively. This does not imply an adversarial relationship with other management team members, but the nature of security functions,

Management Activity	Group Size	Frequency	Duration
External top-level meetings	8	2/year	4 h
Internal top-level meetings	10	2/year	16 h
Internal top-level teleconference	10	52/year	1 h
Policy group	12	12/year	16 h
Policy review	8	2/year	4 h
Audit review	12	12/year	4 h
Testing group	n/a	Continuous	n/a
Testing review	10	4/year	4 h
Technical safeguards	n/a	Continuous	n/a
Technical review	12	4/year	8 h
Personnel group	n/a	Continuous	n/a
Personnel review	4	2/year	2 h
Incident handling	n/a	Continuous	n/a
Incident review	12	4/year	4 h
Emergency management	12	As needed	As needed
Business continuity planning	n/a	Ongoing	n/a
Disaster recovery	n/a	Ongoing	n/a
Strategic incident team	4	Continuous	n/a
Legal group	6	As needed	As needed
Legal review	12	As needed	As needed
Physical security group	6	12/year	8 h
Physical security review	12	1/year	8 h
Facility security groups	6	As needed	As needed
Awareness group	n/a	Continuous	n/a
Awareness review board	4	12/year	2 h
Insurance and risk transfer	6	As needed	As needed
Internal technical review board	12	12/year	8 h
External technical review board	12	4/year	8 h
Internal management advisory	6	2/year	4 h
External management advisory	12	1/year	16 h
Zoning boards	12	12/year	2 h

like audit functions, demands that independence be maintained for objective evaluation to take place. Also:

- The evidence over a long time frame indicates that insiders are involved in 80% of the losses encountered in information system attacks. Many people misstate this statistic as indicating that 80% of attacks involve insiders, but in fact a relatively small number of attacks result in most of the real harm, and many of these involve high-level insiders.
- In case after case, security decisions blocked by executives were used to cover up executive misdeeds. It is critical that a top-level decision-maker act as an independent reviewer of security-related issues, just as it is critical that financial auditors report directly to top executives and be independent of those who can move funds.
- In case after case, mid-level managers or technical people decided that security enhancements were infeasible because of difficulties in getting

them through their management, even though they thought they were the right things to do. In one case, a major single point of failure for an entire enterprise was identified in a security review but not passed to top management because a mid-level reviewer determined that it would likely be rejected. This should never happen when a CISO is in charge of these processes but it is common in those without a high-level CISO.

■ Regulations like Sarbanes–Oxley require that top management attest to the true state of the enterprise's financial well-being with criminal sanctions for failures to report. A failure such as the information system collapse that caused all Comair flights to be canceled over the Christmas weekend in 2004, stranding 30,000 passengers for days, clearly demonstrates the sort of risks at hand.

1.5   Should the CISO, CPO, CSO, or Others be Combined?

In many cases, enterprises consider joint positions for the chief information security officer (CISO); the chief of corporate physical security, sometimes called the chief security officer (CSO); or the chief privacy officer (CPO). There are situations in which these positions can be joined, but great care should be taken in understanding the implications of this combination. Given the complexity of the CISO job, there is little free time left for this member of the management team. Unless there is a mitigating circumstance, overloading the CISO position will cause degraded job performance. Here are some exceptions:

■ If the nature of the business is such that the physical security function predominantly covers only information systems and assets, combining the functions may be sensible.

■ If there is a large inventory control or production component to the business, or if personnel protection is nontrivial, then a physical security lead is most likely needed for the enterprise, and to expect the combined position to do the job as well would be a mistake.

■ Placing the CSO function underneath the CISO or the CISO underneath the CSO is also a mistake unless there is such a large component of one and small component of the other that they can be conjoined without affecting performance.

■ If there is no physical security lead, use the CISO's physical security group as the enterprise lead for physical security associated with information systems.

■ If physical security is handled by local facilities personnel, a subordinate to the CISO should coordinate facilities security for information technology in a matrix management arrangement with the local facility owner.

The CPO role is usually highly focused in privacy-related issues and deals largely with the enormous global complexity associated with privacy regulations. This is largely a legal-department issue and is most often handled that way. While the CPO is a critical enterprise function, the complexity and technical detail level is high and it is, in practice, infeasible to keep fully up to date in these issues while also operating such a broad management function, except in cases where the enterprise is highly localized.

1.5.1 Where Should the CISO Be in the Corporate Structure?

An independent top-level position for the CISO is necessary. This may be a side box adjacent to the CEO's office, the board of directors, or the audit committee. It may be placed within the chief counsel's office, but this will be problematic for the legal department. Or the CISO can be a member of the management committee.

1.6 Budgets and Situations

Some industry sources provide gross budget numbers for information protection, but these have little relevance to the actual budgeting process in most enterprises. Different enterprises use different budgeting processes, from central committee-determined project approaches to hierarchical budgets derived from top management projections and to emergency funding for critical projects in response to incidents. The lack of clear guidance and figures for information security budgets belies a lack of clear understanding of the protection process and a lack of meaningful ways to codify true costs. A good top-level CISO who is in charge of the process should be able to generate meaningful financial metrics within a year or so of taking over the position if adequate cooperation is provided. But these will almost always be cost metrics with performance associated with fulfillment of organizational goals rather than income.

1.6.1 Direct Budget for the CISO

Although no attempt will be made here to create the overall budget associated with the protection process, some things are clear just from the governance requirements identified. Funding on the order of $2–3M per year for the CISO and top-level team will be required to cover salaries and overhead. These are critical components of overall enterprise protection, and trying to cut corners here is a mistake. The CISO team typically also has $2–3M in discretionary funds available for meetings, improvements, travel, initial tests of new security technologies, expert consultant time, keeping up-to-date, and other similar items. This does not include any of the funds required to run security operations. It only covers management of the process at the enterprise level.

1.6.2 Identifiable Costs

To effectively measure the information protection program in terms of costs and performance, costs must be identified and performance measures put in place. Although hidden costs remain, it is important to track identifiable costs from all sources to get a handle on what they are and where they come from.

Each enterprise and many business units within enterprises make their own decisions about how to budget and pay for protection. Many enterprises ignore some of the protection issues or consolidate them within other areas. Ownership of issues varies widely, but as a rule, if they are not otherwise owned, they end up owned by the CISO. Budgets for widely used common items like antivirus solutions or forensics tools often start in some niche area but ultimately end up borne on an enterprisewide basis. These budgets and the functions they pay for should end up owned by the CISO so they can be properly accounted for, optimized over time, and eliminated or changed if appropriate.

Some costs are readily identified. For example, a typical security awareness program costs from $10 to $100 per user per year, not including trainee and team leader time. But budget sources for training and awareness vary from company to company. Some companies track training time to an overhead account within each user's organization, some use charge-back systems to account for the time, and others roll training time into general overhead budgets or project budgets for the project generating the training requirement. Some companies have separate training budgets and treat educational efforts associated with specialized information security experts as part of the benefits package. Regardless of how the budget process works, it takes money to perform these functions, and over the long run that money must come from some identified funding processes in order for the program to become normalized within the enterprise.

A typical centralized cost is a corporate license to a virus or spam defenses and other similar content controls. One example of the advantage of centralization in the CISO's office was played out in a recent decision by a large enterprise to switch vendors. The savings amounted to $500,000 per year in reduced cost for a solution that the protection testing and change control team found to be otherwise equivalent to its competitor. The process put in place before there was a CISO to make this enterprise-level decision was based on a brand name and involved no significant testing of alternatives. It was operated for several years out of the CIO's office without any attempt to optimize. Several other similar steps by the same CISO have resulted in millions of dollars of cost reductions while improving protection effectiveness and regulatory compliance stance.

Another critical area that can only be handled centrally is business continuity and disaster recovery planning. The budgets in this area can be very substantial, usually amounting to the creation of a redundant capability for all critical business functions. Amounts in the range of $20M per year for business continuity planning and related facilities are commonplace. The coordination required for this involves everything from holding scenario development exercises with top management to regular practice of every component and the plan as a whole. These pay off only when disasters strike, but without these efforts, business collapse is inevitable.

In making up a list of costs, the structures used for identifying protection processes above are used. For each area, determine what costs are tracked, who pays for what, how much they pay, how they do it, and what costs remain hidden. These can be listed in a table like the following table. The example provided is from a newly created business unit in a large financial institution. Some costs are expected to be double in the first year because of the use of consultants for program development.

Area	Budget Source	Annual Costs	Hidden Costs
Security management	CISO	$5M	n/a
Policy	CISO	$200K	Churn, time, morale
Standards	CISO	$200K	Churn, time
Procedures	Distributed	$200K	Churn, time
Documentation	Distributed	Unbudgeted	All hidden
Security Auditing	Audit or CISO	$150K	Churn, time
Protection Testing	Varies	$450K	Time
Technology	Distributed	$5M	Churn, time, morale
Personnel (training)	HR	$300K	Time
Incident handling	Varies	Unbudgeted	Churn, time
Legal	Legal	$250K	All hidden
Physical	CSO	Provided	Time, morale
Knowledge	Benefits	$2K/course	n/a
Awareness	Varies	$250K	User time
Organizational	CISO	Unbudgeted	Time, stress
Business lifecycles	Business Units	Unbudgeted	Many of them
People lifecycles	HR	Unbudgeted	Time, morale
System lifecycles	System owners	Unbudgeted	Time, churn
Data lifecycles	Data owners	Unbudgeted	Time, churn
Deterrence	CISO	Unbudgeted	Time, churn
Prevention	Varies	$100K (HW)	Time, morale
Detection	Varies	$100K (HW)	Time, morale
Reaction	Varies	$1M (IDS team	Time, morale
Adaptation	Owners	Unbudgeted	Churn, time
Integrity	Data owner	Unbudgeted	Churn, time
Availability	System owners	$20M (BCP)	Churn, time
Confidentiality	Data owner	Unbudgeted	Churn, time
Use control	Business owner	$5M (IdM)	Time, morale
Accountability	Business owner	$5M (retention)	Time, morale
Risk management	Enterprise	$500K	Error costs
Insurance (transfer)	Enterprise	Unbudgeted	Policy limits
Losses	Enterprise	Unbudgeted	Churn, time, morale
Mitigation	CISO / owners	Unbudgeted	Churn, time, morale
Public relations	Communication	Unbudgeted	Stress, morale
Brand	Communication	Unbudgeted	Stress
TOTALS	**N/A**	**$43.2M**	**N/A**

As this example shows, costs vary across different functions. Costs of $5M per year for retention of records is more than many enterprises spend in information protection budget, and the $20M in disaster recovery costs vary greatly depending on the business and the nature of the operation.

1.7 Enforcement and Appeals Processes

The enforcement and appeals process is perhaps the trickiest area of information security governance. While physical force, like the use of guards for escorting newly terminated employees, may ultimately be involved in security processes, clearly this is to be avoided where possible. This is particularly problematic between executives who may not buy into information protection ideas quickly.

1.7.1 Top Management Buy-In and Support

A goal of any effective information protection program from the standpoint of the CISO is that the top management team embrace and assist in the effort in a highly cooperative process. This is yet another reason that the CISO must be part of that management team or closely linked to its members. Without this sort of cooperative arrangement, the tensions and disputes that ultimately arise will cause the program to fail, power struggles will dominate the best interests of the enterprise, and business will suffer.

It is fundamental and yet often inadequately understood or stated that the goal of information protection should be to optimize business results. On this all top management should agree. But one of the major challenges of the CISO is providing adequate understanding to other top management team members to gain their support in initiatives. If a policy has an enforcement mechanism that results in an override by a management team member, the CISO should agree on the override and it should be a sound business decision, not a reaction to a newspaper article or a feeling of some sort. This implies a level of communication and maturity that is sometimes hard to find, and a common basis for judgments.

1.7.2 Power and Influence and Managing Change

Dispute resolution often comes down to who has what power and influence, and how that power and influence is applied. Different organizations also apply power in different ways. The direct application of power is considered uncouth in many organizations, while other organizations are run by fear with power exercised directly and brutally. The successful CISO must have the necessary elements of power and influence to get the job done, must be able to apply them properly, and must be able to extend them to team members to get their jobs done. Many disputes can be avoided by proper influence and clear communications. Power and influence are wielded in many ways.

The effective CISO has to learn to manage change within the organization. This involves understanding how to effectively communicate the right information to the right people at the right time and providing the proper motivations to allow others to embrace or at least allow the changes to take place. The change process and how it is managed is a key governance issue, particularly for organizations in transition and newly anointed CISOs making their mark.

1.7.3 Responses to Power and Influence

The use of power and influence can result in compliance, identification, or internalization.

- **Compliance** is associated with forced behavior with no choice. This produces resentment and may also result in malicious compliance. Work-to-rule responses are common in compliance situations where workers are very careful to follow every rule to the letter and with great care, thus dramatically reducing output but still not breaking any rules.
- **Identification** comes from liking the idea or the person who is asking for the behavior. It results in behaviors that, with a little awareness and support, get done reliably and without resentment.
- **Internalization** is associated with the adoption of the influence as their own. The individual takes ownership of the idea and works not only to support it but to improve and personalize it.

The objective in most cases should be to go beyond compliance. Identification results in increased adoption and is far better than compliance. Internalization is still better in some cases, but in a security context, internalization is not always most effective or desired, because adopting an idea may lead to personalization and this can lead to non-compliance, particularly when the standards are very specific and inflexible. Regulatory compliance and contract issues are examples where identification may be better. Measurement of the difference between compliance, identification, and internalization is important to the success of a program but may be problematic, given available measurement techniques.

1.7.4 Other Power Issues

The independence of the information protection function is critical. While friendly persuasion is a valuable approach, force must be available to allow the CISO access to the resources required to do the job, independent of, and without interference from or knowledge of others. The power relationship between the CISO and the rest of the company must be designed to allow protection to be effective. It is a fundamental separation of duties issue as identified by GASSP and the OECD guidelines, and it is necessary in order to assure independent evaluation for the executives who have to attest to conditions that put the enterprise at risk. Force must be an option to handle situations without other options, but it must be used wisely, be transparent to authorized reviewers, and be properly attributed so that responsibility can be maintained.

Force is necessary when time is of the essence, and cooperation is not given or is not feasible because those in control are subjects of the process. Force may have to be covert to be effective, suggesting substantial complications in its use. Both overt and covert forces should be available under proper control. Covert investigations typically involve physical devices and logical mechanisms, and thus physical security elements are involved in the process. Covert force generally ends up involving the legal team unless the legal team is the subject of the process, in which case it involves the CEO and external counsel. Investigations of the CISO are typically done by the CEO in conjunction with outside counsel and private investigation firms.

There are typically inflection points in the exercise of power to achieve large-scale changes. Most people try to avoid the use of overt power because of its tendency to produce compliance rather than internalization. But internalization takes time and, in many cases, time is of the essence in information protection. Most CISOs try to work cooperatively except in cases of dire need. They try to bank goodwill as an approach to achieving identification with the large-scale changes desired for the enterprise and to allow them to continue to be effective when they have to use force. There is a tension between the use of force and goodwill, and goodwill wanes with time unless propped up on an ongoing basis. So a key skill for the successful CISO is knowing when the severity of the situation warrants the use of force and when goodwill is more important than resolving an immediate situation with force.

1.8 The Control System

The enterprise information protection control system is comprised of all of the security-related actions taken by, information gathered by, and decisions made by all of the groups and individuals discussed here. Each security function has responsibilities and tasks to carry out. Meetings are designed to provide control over these functions. The power exerted through the groups and the information they bring back form the actuators and sensors of the control system at the management level. The decisions taken by the groups and individuals in those groups form the analytical part of the control system and should be designed to meet the control objectives of the group and, by implication, of the enterprise.

Within these control systems, there are more in-depth and detailed control systems. For example, when a network zoning request shows up at the zoning board, it has to be passed through technical and nontechnical experts in other groups for evaluation, and actions on the request have to be documented through their systems. A record is created reflecting the life of the project that involves records and decision processes at every level and in every area appropriate to the need. Each of these groups and the actions of their members are themselves control systems acting within the zoning process and, of course, also within their own functional areas. Ultimately, every individual is a control system that participates with others in other control systems, forming the overall set of controls that operate the enterprise protection program.

1.8.1 Metrics

For any control system to work, it must have ways to measure inputs from sensors and lower level control systems and to be measured by higher-level control systems. Measurements come in many forms. Some measurements may be turned into metrics to allow them to be compared with other measurements. In many cases, metrics are created for comparison but have little to do with the control objectives of the systems that use them. These are a waste of time and effort, and tend to obfuscate the control issues. Meaningful metrics have utility in meeting the control objectives of the control system. Two sorts of metrics must be generated by each control system to be effective in context: (1) metrics that allow local control objectives to be met, and (2) metrics that are inputs to higher-level control systems and that are meaningful for achieving the higher level control objectives.

1.8.1.1   Costs

Generally, costs are critical metrics for business-related control systems. At the top level, costs are typically rolled up for accounting purposes and associated with a classification system to allow management to understand what they are spending money on, and what they are getting for that money. While security costs are hard to track because of hidden costs, indirect costs, cost center accounting practices, and so forth, tracking costs is really the easiest part of security metrics. Costs are typically tracked in only one form, monetary units, and they are fully commensurable with each other and fungible, even if, from a budget standpoint, they may not appear to be either commensurable or fungible.

1.8.1.2   Performance

The hard thing to get a handle on is meaningful metrics for performance. Metrics that are useful at the governance level are those that provide measurements of the effectiveness of the comprehensive approach. The Capability Maturity Model for Security (CMM-SEC) provides a way to measure progress of an overall program in terms of normalization into enterprise operations. It associates levels 0 through 5 (none, initial, repeatable, defined, managed, and optimizing) with each of 11 process areas and 11 organizational issues mapped against risk management, engineering processes, assurance, and coordination to provide an overall picture of the maturity of the information protection function within an enterprise. The ISO 17799 standard is often used as a basis of comparison by qualitative scores ranging from poor to excellent for each of the areas covered. Similar scoring with GASSP or the elements of the overall program also work. Roll-ups of these scores are often presented as a status and measurement of the overall program. For example, if out of 50 high-valued systems, separation of duties was poor in 35, fair in 10, and good in 5, separation of duties might be ranked as poor for the enterprise.

1.8.1.3   Time

CISOs normally provide top management with a plan intended to go from where they start to where they want to be in some time frame. They measure progress against those goals over time and sometimes alter the plan to suit changed assumptions or conditions. Once the overall protection program reaches stability, it may be run on a maintenance basis with efficiency measurements dominating progress measurements. Progress is typically measured by the CISO and independently validated by periodic information protection posture assessments (IPPAs). An IPPA is often performed at the start of a CISO's tenure to get initial values for the program and set prioritized objectives over time.

1.8.1.4   Lower-Level Metrics

Measurements from lower-level control systems feed into higher-level control systems eventually reaching the CISO's measurement process by providing information that is relevant to governance issues. But most of the groups that provide this information to the CISO operate within more detailed areas. As a result, these groups tend to think in terms of the work they are doing instead of the issues addressed in top-level governance. It is the task of the CISO to:

- Define metrics that are meaningful to the top-level governance issues
- Identify which metrics are to be delivered in what format by each group
- Provide groups with what they need to generate those metrics
- Turn these lower-level metrics into CISO metrics

Risk	Risk Management	Engineering	Assurance	Coordination
Administer controls				
Assess impact				
Assess risk				
Assess threat				
Assess vulnerability				
Assurance argument				
Coordinate security				
Monitor posture				
Provide input				
Specify needs				
Verify and validate				

As an example, suppose the CISO wants to measure the maturity of the incident response process according to the CMM-SEC methodology in order to provide a metric on that element of the overall program. This measurement goes across risk management, engineering, assurance, and coordination, and involves ratings for each identified area. Answers should be in the range 0–5 for none-optimizing.

A roll-up metric can then be generated by weighting each cell in the matrix and producing a weighted average. Program roll-up can be done by normalizing and weighting program elements to provide an overall weighted average.

1.9   How Long Will It Take?

Hierarchical control systems tend to have more and faster actuators, sensors, and control mechanisms at lower levels of the hierarchy than at higher levels. As a result, time scales in information protection range from microseconds at the lowest levels to years at the strategic management level. One of the goals of an effective control system is that decisions with high consequences requiring in-depth analysis can be made in longer time frames than decisions with low consequence requiring little analysis. This provides the added observation, orientation, decision, and action (OODA) time required to get better answers deployed at larger scales for higher values. Information protection sometimes requires large-scale efforts be undertaken at a fast tempo, but a well designed information protection control system does not need to react to events as much as it needs to adapt to changes in the environment and the enterprise direction.

To get from an ad hoc system of controls in an environment that is not structured for proper governance and control to an efficiently working governance and control structure takes a long time. Even if everything were instantly put in place from a systems standpoint, the people and processes take time to develop and adapt. There are life cycles associated with businesses, people, systems, and data that cannot be pushed too hard without causing them to break and the overall system to fail. One of the useful ways to measure time in terms of governance is to identify how long it typically takes to move from one level of performance in the governance metrics to the next level, assuming that adequate support in terms of power, influence, cooperation, and funding are present. If these are not present, the times are of course longer.

In typical IPPA studies, three time frames are considered. The urgent time frame is typically from immediate to 6 months and involves high consequence situations inducible by glaring vulnerabilities and subject to threats with demonstrated capabilities and intents to attack. In the tactical time frame of 6 to 18 months, the time typically required to complete a substantial infrastructure project, governance issues are typically addressed in terms of moving from the "none" or "initial" level of the CMM-SEC metrics to the "repeatable" or "defined" level. Similarly, ratings in ISO 17799 and GAISP metrics can be improved by one step in this time frame. In the strategic time frame of 18 months to 3 years from the start of the effort, enterprises can move from the "defined" to "managed" level of the CMM-SEC and up another few levels in other metrics. Once objective levels are achieved, they are typically suitable to ongoing operations, and the protection posture is kept up to date over time.

Changes involving people take from a few months for large-scale awareness programs to four or more years associated with educational processes. Mergers and acquisitions produce additional processes reflective of the enterprisewide process and typically take from six to eighteen months to integrate into the overall information protection program. They operate in an ongoing integration cycle starting when they become part of the enterprise. Breakups do not typically create large-scale governance changes, however, as expertise moves from place to place, lost functions must be replaced, and this typically takes some time and effort. It is common for a stable protection program to restabilize in six months after a large-scale breakup.

Major changes in system security typically correspond to system life cycles if done cost effectively. For systems with long life cycles, these changes usually involve external protective devices. Minor system changes happen all the time with time frames limited only by the research, development, testing, and change control process. Data changes are almost universally made over short time frames depending only on the time required to make and validate the changes.

Startup of large-scale information protection governance and control programs is often problematic because of inadequate expertise or inadequate control over expertise in place. A program can be created from scratch and brought up to a reasonable level of performance in two to three years following from an IPPA. This start-up challenge can sometimes be reduced by using external experts. Outsourcing of critical high-level functions is feasible for periods of time, particularly when building a program up; however, in the long run the level of expertise required for key positions makes it expensive to outsource and may make governance more difficult. Key areas where outsourcing works well are likely to include:

- The staff assistant can typically be outsourced but is easiest to find.
- An awareness and knowledge lead can be brought in part-time to start the program. Replace this person with an inside staff member in a year.
- Consultants can be used on select high-consequence reviews if desired, but as internal testing leads they are too expensive.
- A security audit lead is often brought in from the internal audit department. External expertise is usually used for protection posture assessments or to augment audit processes on a case-by-case basis.
- A policy, standards, and procedures lead, or an initial development group is probably better outsourced than internally created. Eventually, an insider should take over the lead.
- As an interim step outsourced private investigation background check firms can be used for select augmentation purposes.

Whole programs can be outsourced in some cases. Even the CISO can be outsourced for some enterprises for some time. But this is not a long-term solution. It should only be used to bridge between CISOs or for program start-up when no internal CISO is available, and a CISO and program must be built.

1.10 Summary

The CISO governs enterprise information protection by a combination of power and influence. This involves the creation and operation of institutions that cross all organizational boundaries and involve business functions, operations, and assurance processes at all levels. In each area of involvement, the CISO exerts control, gets feedback, and acts to continue operations within the desired control envelope. At the overall level, business functions push operational needs that push assurance processes, and the CISO must also control the process at this level in order to be effective.

Different people in different roles interact with information and the information control system in different ways. Pure business functions like the policy team, HR, Legal, and the risk management team interact with pure operations functions like the testing and change management team and incident response team, and with pure assurance functions like the audit team, education and awareness teams, and documentation specialists. But mixed teams also exist to bridge between these areas, like project teams, technology teams, and project management teams. The CISO crosses all of these boundaries in order to assure that the enterprise prospers and that it can effectively deal with the risks inherent in the efficiencies gained by modern information technology within the enterprise.

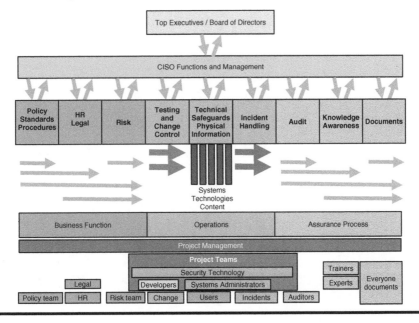

1.10. Summary

Chapter 2

Drill-Down

This drill-down describes many of the more complex issues identified in the structural part of the guidebook in far greater detail. It describes the complex diagrams in more depth and in most cases drills down to another level providing lists of issues associated with each element identified. We start with the comprehensive picture of information protection from above.

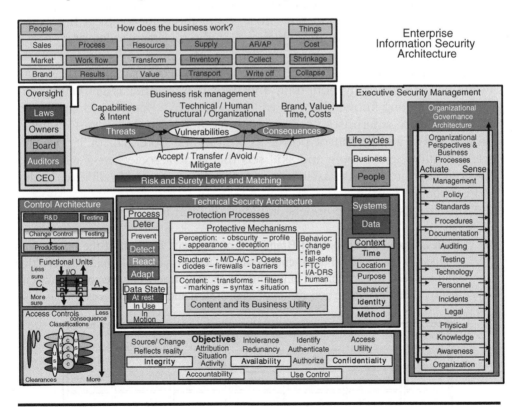

This is broken down into how the business works, oversight, business risk management, executive security management with its organizational perspectives and business processes, control architecture with its protection objectives, access controls, change controls, and functional units, technical security architecture and its interaction with life cycles, attack and defense processes, contextual issues, and data states, and protective mechanisms with its elements of perception, structure, content, and behavior. Each area will be investigated in more depth.

2.1 How the Business Works

Each "business" is unique in what it does, and yet businesses share some features with each other.

For example, all businesses involve people and things.

- **People** have to be dealt with in terms of their value in doing things and have to be paid to keep working.
- **Things** have inherent value, are inventoried and tracked, and get bought, sold, lost, and stolen.

Because most businesses deal with currency, this is certainly an important element of the business modeling process, but the value of most businesses is an order of magnitude or more higher than the inventory value of its assets. This difference is, in one form or another, the information value of the enterprise. Enterprises also value different things. For example, educational institutions are generally nonprofit, and their main output is graduating students with lifelong knowledge that will help them live better and help society prosper. Military enterprises produce the force needed to help exert influence through direct application of power as well as the potential for its use that deters conflicts and people and skill sets that benefit society as a whole, but they can also produce devastation and large-scale loss of life, liberty, health, and property.

Most businesses can be understood at some level in terms of the following:

Sales, market, and brand: Brand is a reputational element of the information value of a business and represents a critical factor in sales. Information protection failures tend to harm brand, but claims of security rarely enhance brand substantially. Brand is vital to generation of leads, sales, and ease of success in business.

People	How does the business work?					Things
Sales	Process	Resource	Supply	AR/AP	Infrastruc.	Cost
Market	Work flow	Transform	Inventory	Collect	Services	Shrink
Brand	Results	Value	Transport	Write off	Users	Collapse

Marketing and the markets that a business operate in dictate to a large extent the aspects of information protection that apply and the tolerance for risk and need for protection. Sales are more directly related to income. All of these also involve business processes that are key to success, and failures in these processes lead to anything from release of critical competitive information such as pricing or customer details to incorrect pricing or inability to process orders. Any of these can be catastrophic to some businesses.

Process, work flow, and results: Business processes are critical to business survival, and, increasingly, they are highly automated. Attacks on workflows can be highly destructive and cause subtle effects such as the chance for unauthorized individuals to cause unauthorized changes to business processes, grant themselves access or monies, destroy logistics, and otherwise disrupt business operations.

Resources, transforms, and value: Resources are transformed into value through processes. For example, land is transformed into gold through extraction processes, chemicals are transformed into medicines through chemical processes, and raw data is transformed into competitive intelligence through analytical processes. These processes are fundamental to how many businesses operate, and failures in theses processes lead to failures in the ability of the enterprise to produce value.

Supply, inventory, and transport: Many enterprises take supplies of some sort and move them from place to place to produce value. Wholesalers and retailers move supplies from suppliers through warehouses and storefronts to consumers or customers, whereas many companies have internal logistics processes that support their operations in one way or another. Disruptions in the supply and logistics process can cause anything from military campaigns to businesses to fall apart.

Accounts receivable (AR), accounts payable (AP), collections, and write-offs: With the exception of purely cash businesses, all businesses have accounts receivable and payable, collection processes, and write-offs. These processes are critical to cash flow and business operations as well as profitability and customer relations. Failures in these processes can cause businesses to lose the confidence of their customers, to offend customers, to be stolen from in large quantities, and to be unable to meet payroll or other obligations and go bankrupt. Other elements of the financial systems of businesses are also important in much the same way and are subject to malicious attack for their direct financial value.

Infrastructures, services, and users: Infrastructure is used along with services and applications to meet the desires and needs of users. The value of infrastructure consists in the utility of the services provided to users. If infrastructures or the services they support fail, businesses obviously suffer. These services also support content that may have inherent value, lose value with exposure or time, or otherwise be affected by failures in protection. At the same time, their utility is determined by the usability of these services.

Cost, shrinkage, and collapse: Costs and changes in costs and cost structure, shrinkage (loss and theft of inventory), and, ultimately, collapse of markets or businesses effect enterprises in a wide range of ways.

These and other business functions can be codified in terms of business process diagrams, and the elements of the process diagrams can be associated with failure conditions producing losses as a function of the durations of failures. Information technology and its role in supporting these business processes can be codified by indicating which processes that technology interacts with and how losses of integrity, availability, confidentiality, use control, and accountability can impact those processes. These, then, are the depictions of the business that help to understand information and information technology-related risks from a business perspective.

2.2   The Security Oversight Function

Oversight is the critical governance function provided by top management relating to information protection, and it is fundamental to proper operation of a protection program. It is the job of oversight to ensure that proper duties to protect are put in place, that the management measures the effectiveness of the protection program in fulfilling those duties, and that management adapts the protection program to meet those duties.

> **Laws:** Laws and regulations define the legally mandated duties to protect associated with jurisdictions. All laws of all jurisdictions in which an enterprise operates have to be considered to make prudent determinations about duties to protect.
>
> **Owners:** The owners are the ones hurt by bad management decisions, and they need to ensure that their investment is not lost by electing proper boards of directors. For public companies, there are regulatory assurances to support the public owners, so that they do not have to get involved in the details of selections to reasonably protect their investments, but this lack of direct control by owners is often reflected in the frauds we see around the world. Owners of privately held firms are directly responsible for the disposition of their assets and for proper protection, and they directly suffer from poor decisions in this regard.
>
> **Board:** The board of directors is legally and morally responsible to ensure that the CEO and other officers are doing their jobs and have the ability to define additional duties to protect, in keeping with their responsibilities. They also have oversight responsibility to act on behalf of the shareholders to ensure that shareholder value is protected.
>
> **Auditors:** Auditors are tasked with providing independent and objective feedback to the shareholders, board of directors, CEO, and others on the effectiveness of the protection program in fulfilling its duty to protect, within the risk tolerance parameters set by management.
>
> **CEO:** The CEO is responsible for day-to-day control over the enterprise and, as part and parcel of this responsibility, for protecting shareholder value, identifying the duties to protect, ensuring that those duties are carried out, and measuring the performance of those duties to allow adequate control in situations that warrant improvement, keeping costs as low as possible, without undertaking inappropriate levels of risk.

In concert, these elements comprise the oversight function of enterprise information protection and define the duty to protect.

2.2.1 Duty to Protect

Individuals in organizations also have duties to protect various aspects of doing business. Duties stem from three general areas: externally imposed duties, internally imposed duties, and duties associated with contracts.

2.2.1.1 Externally Imposed Duties

Legal and regulatory mandates are derived from laws, regulations, protective orders, judicial determinations, and ordinances at all jurisdictional levels. There are generally three classes of these duties: (1) those associated with all businesses in jurisdictions, (2) those associated with specific types of businesses involving special duties like public health and safety duties of drug or chemical manufacturers, and (3) fiduciary duties to shareholders by officers to protect and increase the value of the shareholder investments.

2.2.1.2 Internally Imposed Duties

Companies often decide to protect private information, safety of workers, release of information to third parties, and other similar information or assets beyond the levels imposed by government. When these decisions are codified in any form, including but not limited to normal operating procedures and processes, documented practices, or policies, they obtain the force of a legal obligation. These self-imposed duties can be the basis of legal actions against the corporation. A good example was a privacy policy published on a Web site by a large Internet service provider. They did not follow their self-imposed privacy policy, got sued for disclosure of information, and lost $1 million in the process. If they had no such policy, they would have had no such duty to protect and would have had no liability. Trade secrets, copyrights, and patents are important examples of intellectual property with self-imposed duties to protect.

2.2.1.3   Contractual Duties

Contractual obligations are legally binding obligations voluntarily taken on as part of doing business. They typically include things like safe harbor agreements, confidentiality and nondisclosure agreements, trade secret agreements, licensing agreements for patented or copyrighted material, and almost anything else that the parties wish to codify in a legal agreement as part of the terms and conditions of doing business.

2.3   Risk Management and What to Protect

Risk management transforms duty to protect into what to protect and how well to protect it, selects between risk acceptance, transfer, avoidance, and mitigation, and, for risk mitigation, attempts to match surety of mitigation with desired risk reduction.

Risks are generally formed from the combination of threats, vulnerabilities, and consequences. Threats, including nature and accidents as well as individual actors and groups, possibly acting in concert, exploit sequences of vulnerabilities to induce consequences.

2.3.1 Risk Evaluation

Risks have to be identified and evaluated to be managed. The objective of risk evaluation is to identify event sequences with potentially serious negative consequences based on the business model.

2.3.1.1   Consequences

Consequences are identified from the business model and rated, typically, into low, medium, and high levels. Low consequence is considered typical of

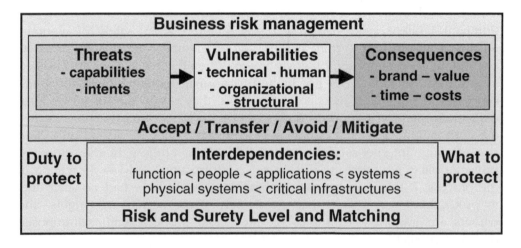

business risks like slip-and-fall accidents and similar readily insurable events. Medium risks tend to have serious business impact and include public relations problems, loss of substantial amounts of trust or money, inability to perform on select important contracts, and so forth. High consequences tend to involve loss of life, great harm to the environment, collapse of the business, or jail time to executives. Consequences are very specific to the organization; however, they tend to group into issues of (1) brand or reputation, (2) value, which has a variety of financial implications, ranging from loss of cash to destruction of stock, to loss of information value for periods of time, (3) time lost because people were not effective at their jobs or the business missed opportunities, and (4) costs, i.e., the direct costs of dealing with the incident and its aftermath.

2.3.1.2   Threats

For event sequences involving medium or high consequences, threats are assessed with increasing attention and in more detail, the higher the consequences. As threats are identified, their capabilities and intents are taken into consideration in assessing the threats. Threats have capabilities and intents. Capabilities include but are not limited to funding, location, attack mechanisms available, group size, available resources, skill sets, training levels, allies, and access. Intents are harder to identify with specificity; however, they are typically assessed in light of group history, motives, group behaviors, group rewards, typical targets, leadership, and declared objectives.

2.3.1.3   Vulnerabilities

For systems with identified high or medium consequences whose threats have been assessed as having the capabilities and intents to induce those consequences, vulnerability analysis and mitigation is considered. Vulnerabilities and the paths attackers take to exploit vulnerabilities were described earlier in general terms. They tend to include technical vulnerabilities most commonly associated with computer security, human vulnerabilities that are covered under a variety of topic areas in the psychological literature, structural vulnerabilities that have to do with overall network and infrastructure architecture and dependencies, and organizational vulnerabilities that have to do with weaknesses in the way things are organized and how people interact with each other within the structure.

Vulnerabilities are typically assessed by a testing process of some sort and ranked by criticality and severity in context. The problem with most vulnerability assessments in use today is that they are undertaken as independent efforts and not within the proper enterprise context. They find many vulnerabilities in low-valued systems, fail to properly evaluate their implications, and indicate mitigation that is more expensive and of a higher order than would be necessary if the task was more properly done. As a rule, for an efficient protection program, vulnerability assessment should be done only selectively and as directed by results of consequence assessment followed by threat assessment.

2.3.1.4   Interdependencies and Risk Aggregations

Interdependencies are far more complex in information technology than in most other systems because of the implementation of information systems over vast distances and the short time frames associated with the transfer of information over those distances.

2.3.1.4.1   Interdependencies

Business utility, or function, depends on a large hierarchy of mechanisms. People dependencies start with users, administrators, and support personnel that use systems and keep them functioning. These people depend, in turn, on application programs, data files, and input and output systems for their interactions with information technology. These applications work through systems infrastructures that include operating systems, libraries, and configurations. The system infrastructures often depend on distant application infrastructures such as domain name services, identity management systems, back-end processing facilities, and the protocols that are used to communicate with these capabilities. The application infrastructure operates over physical infrastructures that include computing platforms, networks, wires, routing protocols, and accessibility to all these elements. The physical information infrastructure then depends on power, cooling, heat, air, communications infrastructure, governments and political stability, environmental conditions and controls, supplies, and people as well as their safety and health. In this complex chain of interdependencies, any fault can cause systemic failure unless the fault is covered by some sort of protective mechanism that allows the overall system to continue to function in its presence. Because some of the fault mechanisms, such as computer viruses or unreliable electrical power supply, are active and potentially systemic in nature, subtle and unanticipated consequences occur when inadequate expertise is applied to this issue.

> **Function: Business Utility**
> **People: Administrators / User / Support**
> **Application: Programs, Data, Files, I/O**
> **System infrastructure: OS, Libraries, Configuration**
> **Application Infrastructure: DNS / IdM / Back-end / Protocols**
> **Physical infrastructure: Platforms / Networks / Wires / Routing / Access**
> **Critical infrastructure: Power / Cooling /Heat / Air / Communications / Government / Environment / Supplies / People / Safety / Health**

2.3.1.4.2   Single Points of Failure

There are many cases when a single point of failure goes unnoticed for a large infrastructure, and its eventual failure leads to infrastructurewide collapse. Depending on timeliness issues, this can result in consequences ranging from short-term inconvenience to enterprise collapse. The key to understanding single points of failure comes from interdependency analysis to find the dependency chain of all business functions and failure mode analysis associated with all dependencies. There are two classes of single points of failure, One is any individual system, facility, key individual, or other element of the dependency chain, within a radius of effect associated with the attack mechanisms within the capabilities of the threats identified in threat assessment. The other is common-mode failures.

2.3.1.4.3   Radius-Driven Common-Mode Failures

Different threats have different capabilities. Those capabilities lead to radii of effects. For example, nature brings on large-scale effects like earthquakes and hurricanes. To assert a single point of failure protection, natural effects within reasonably expected and historically supported radii must be taken into account. Redundant data centers in the same earthquake zone cannot support the claim that no single point of failure exists, because a single earthquake can cause all of them to fail. Redundancy within a single building will not withstand a single explosion at that building, and this is within the threat profile of any substantial enterprise.

2.3.1.4.4   Other Sorts of Common-Mode Failures

Common-mode failures are failures that result from commonalities between systems or components. Anything that systems have in common and that can fail will be subject to common-mode failures. The only way to eliminate common-mode failures is to use diversity. An example of a widely exploited common-mode failure is the use of large numbers of systems with the same version of the same operating system. A virus that infects those systems tends to do widespread damage. But the operational and cost efficiency of running a single operating system may justify the increased risk of common-mode failures. A diversity approach would be to have multiple implementation of each business function. But, clearly, this at least doubles all development and operational costs, particularly for large-scale systems used for enterprise databases and similar back-end processes. Trade-offs must be made, and selective diversity is typically practiced only after serious analysis is done.

2.3.1.4.5   Key Individuals

A particularly good example of risk aggregation is a single individual who controls a substantial portion of information infrastructure and for whom there is no backup. The trade-offs associated with business failure have to be considered for any small business or small part of a large enterprise. But for any substantial enterprise, such a dependency must be eliminated. Consider the implications if the individual has a heart attack or gets hit by a car.

2.3.2 Risk Treatment

Risk treatment is the process by which risks worthy of attention are managed and risks not worthy of consideration are accepted. A risk treatment plan should be identified for all risks identified.

2.3.2.1 Risk Acceptance

Risk acceptance involves a decision by management to accept a given risk without further mitigation or transfer for a period of time. This happens in two classes of circumstances. For risks that are too low to bother protecting against or for which insurance and due diligence are adequate, risk is accepted. For risks that are to be mitigated but mitigation cannot be done instantaneously or rapid mitigation is too expensive to justify, risks are accepted for periods during which mitigation is undertaken.

2.3.2.2 Risk Avoidance

Risk avoidance is a business strategy in which certain classes of activities or business processes are not undertaken because the risks are too high to justify the return on investment. A typical example is a decision about the maximum value to be placed in a vault, at a site, or on a truck. This strategy avoids the aggregation of risks associated with placing excessive value in one place. Other similar avoidance strategies such as not opening offices in war zones or not doing business in certain localities are commonplace in business.

2.3.2.3 Risk Transfer

Risk transfer for low consequences is usually affordable and reasonable if some level of reasonable and prudent controls are in place. This meets due diligence standards for low-risk systems. Risk transfer for medium and high consequences is rare, expensive, and only justified when the worst-case loss is not sustainable and an adequate outside insurer is willing to take on the risk. This is a strategy that loses in the long run for medium and high risks because insurance companies have to make a lot on each transaction to justify the high consequence of loss and the unknown actuarial nature of the situation.

2.3.2.4 Risk Mitigation

Risk mitigation seeks to reduce the residual risk by using safeguards to eliminate or reduce the likelihood of event sequences that can cause serious negative consequences. This involves reduction of threats, reduction of the link between threats and vulnerabilities, reduction of vulnerabilities, reduction of the link between vulnerabilities and consequences, and reduction of consequences associated with event sequences. All mitigation leaves residual risk that eventually has to be accepted, transferred, or avoided. The question is how much reduction is desired and how much is afforded by the mitigation strategy employed, and at what cost.

2.3.3 What to Protect and How Well

Risk management is the process used by enterprises to turn duty to protect into decisions of what to protect and to what extent they should be protected. It leads to the executive security management function that is tasked with carrying out the duty to protect what should be protected to the extent appropriate to the need.

2.3.4 The Risk Management Space

The risk management process involves many intertwined issues and results in controls appropriate to the risks. As a rule of thumb, starting in the middle

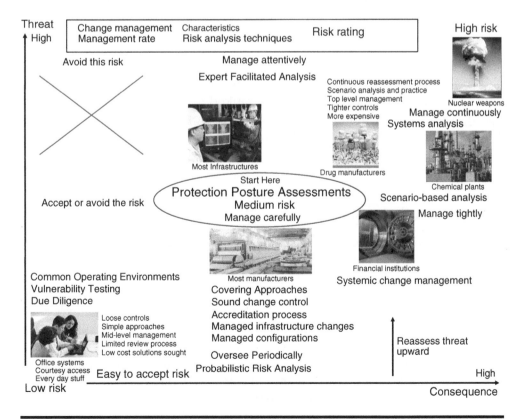

of the risk picture with an information protection posture assessment provides a medium-cost way to get a handle on the overall situation. From there, low, medium-, and high-risk situations are identified, and additional work is done for higher risks. Risk levels lead to management rates and complexity, change management mechanisms, and different risk assessment techniques.

2.3.4.1 Risk Assessment Methodologies and Limitations

There are many risk assessment methodologies. The most popular among them is probabilistic risk assessment (PRA). Unfortunately, this is almost always a poor choice in the information protection field, because PRA assumes that all events are independent, and characterizable in terms of random stochastic processes that do not change substantially over time. When malicious human attackers attack enterprise information systems, they do not follow these rules, so these sorts of assessments tend to be substantially wrong. Furthermore, when planning defenses, many factors such as due diligence, and regulatory and contractual requirements come into play, and are beyond the ability of PRA to help assess defenses. PRA assumes a prevention model as opposed to fusing together deterrence, prevention, detection, reaction, and adaptation. It also has no mechanism for dealing with issues of time or high levels of uncertainty. The result is an approach that is useful for certain simplistic situations but not very useful for governance.

Other risk assessment approaches exist and should be considered; however, the most useful approach in most enterprises does not produce the sorts of results that most risk assessments in other fields are likely to produce. Instead, the end result is a series of ranked consequences with associated and validated threats. After consequences are put in a ranked list, threats are associated with those consequences, and vulnerabilities validated to determine if identified threats could exploit identified vulnerabilities to induce those consequences. Once this is done, a set of validated risks is available. And that is as far as risk assessment can really go.

2.3.4.1.1 Low-Risk Options

For the low-risk end of the spectrum, where most day-to-day users tend to work, due diligence approaches and vulnerability testing are adequate to the risk assessment process. In essence, due diligence with respect to not becoming a hazard are required for any system, and vulnerability testing is a good way to get an initial handle on easily repaired problems. These are inexpensive and suitable to the need. Common operating environments are often used in this environment to save on costs of operation and maintenance. At this end of the spectrum, it is easy to accept risks. As long as there is no really serious consequence associated with failures in these systems, they should be optimized for life-cycle cost and business efficiency.

2.3.4.1.2   Medium-Risk Options

As risks increase, more demands are made on the systems. For medium-risk situations, many things are different. Sound change control and accreditation processes are invoked, configurations are closely managed, and infrastructure supporting the application falls under closer scrutiny and management as well. Probabilistic risk analysis may be used for natural threats, but covering approaches, protection posture assessments, and expert-facilitated analysis are put in place as the threats increase. Although periodic oversight is acceptable at low-threat levels, management must keep tighter reins and review at a higher rate for higher-consequence systems.

2.3.4.1.3   High-Risk Options

When risks reach into the high end, systemic change management comes into play with systemwide testing associated with every significant change. Management rates increase until individual managers are in real-time control over the highest risk systems. Scenario-based analysis becomes increasingly important and, eventually at the highest-risk levels, systems analysis becomes necessary.

2.3.4.1.4   A Systemic Approach to Risk Assessment

A systemic approach at the enterprise level starts with understanding the protection situation. This is typically done with an information protection posture assessment (IPPA). This process operates in the middle of the risk space, has relatively low cost, and provides a high-level view of the situation with respect to consequences and threats. Based on identified consequences and threats, vulnerabilities are also examined, and, when found, mitigation is prioritized based on consequence first, then threat, and sorted into urgent, tactical, and strategic actions. In IPPA, some situations will be identified as low risk and evaluated at a light level, as appropriate. Some situations may be identified as high risk and require additional management attention starting with more in-depth analysis. Medium risks are directly addressed by the IPPA methodology and specific mitigations and timeframes are identified. In addition, IPPA provides metrics on overall program performance.

2.3.4.2   *Matching Surety to Risk*

Generally, higher certainty implies greater costs. So the desire to reduce costs has to be balanced with the desire to reduce risks. As a rule of thumb, as risks increase, the certainty with which they should be mitigated should also increase. Hence, the notion that surety should match risk. Different risk mitigation approaches have different surety levels as indicated under the protective mechanisms area.

Surety, or the certainty with which desired properties of systems can be known to be true, is a continuous range that is most often categorized in sets of levels for convenience. Because more certainty is usually desired for systems with higher risks, surety levels should usually be commensurate with risk levels. In other words, as a rule of thumb, everything that high-valued operations depend on should be high surety, and as the value of the operations decreases, so can the surety of the technology that supports it. Surety can be continuously considered; however, many people find it easier to consider three surety levels.

2.3.4.2.1 Low Risks

In benign environments, low risks operate at acceptable performance levels, but they are not designed for handling medium- or high-valued content. Typically, low risks are the everyday risks similar to those covered by normal business insurance. They are the normal accidents, errors, and omissions with consequences that are not worthy of additional attention beyond normal and prudent practices and due diligence. If a single low-risk system fails so that it never restarts, all data is lost, corrupted, or made available to the news media, and records of what happened are not available, it should have only negligible effect on the enterprise. Risk aggregation comes into play here because failures of large numbers of low-risk systems may, in concert, produce more substantial risk. But as long as these systems are grouped such that computer viruses or similar disruptions cannot aggregate to cause serious business consequences, they are still low risk.

2.3.4.2.2 Low Surety

Low-surety systems are the typical personal computers and rapidly implemented networks that are often used throughout enterprises to support day-to-day low-risk operations such as writing letters and e-mails, preparing studies that are not particularly sensitive, internal Web sites used for general information, and so forth. These systems can be purchased at retail and assembled with minimum effort but cannot be trusted to protect integrity, availability, or confidentiality or provide accountability or user control under malicious attack. Low-surety systems are the everyday computers that are available off the shelf, run with whatever operating system that comes with them, and in their default configurations, and are connected to the rest of the world via the Internet. These systems vary in quality from a protection standpoint, and certainly, this variance can impact operating efficiency, but all such systems are subject to attack and will eventually succumb to attack if the attacker is serious enough about getting to them and they are targeted.

2.3.4.2.3 Medium Risks

They are typically used for manufacturing, transaction processing, banking, critical infrastructure operations, and other controlled environments. Many such systems operate in ISO9000 certified environments as well. Medium risks are substantial enough to cause a need for additional protection. They typically involve consequences that could cause significant implications to shareholder value, that is, the sorts of incidents that trigger the need for mitigation or identification in annual reports under laws such as Sarbanes–Oxley section 404. They include events such as halting manufacturing or causing problems that result in the need for massive recalls, outages that damage the reputation of the enterprise significantly, issues that produce large numbers of disgruntled customers, events that cause closures of facilities or layoffs of employees, and facts that cause business plans to change. Generally, if the CFO or CEO has to get notified, the protection failures fall at least into the medium-risk arena. Medium-surety systems are typified by the systems that run most manufacturing plants and critical infrastructure systems. They tend to use stronger change control, use programmable logic controllers (PLCs) rather than general purpose computers for critical components, are not connected directly to larger networks, and often have regulatory requirements for certification. If these systems go awry, there are generally fail-safe mechanisms like lockouts and dead-man switches that prevent the physical system from continuing to do the potentially hazardous operation. When low-surety systems are used in medium-risk environments, they are a serious hazard unless protected by additional safeguards; therefore, they are generally guarded by PLCs or other similar mechanisms.

2.3.4.2.4 Medium Surety

Medium-surety systems are systems designed to do specific tasks well, engineered for the purpose, well tested under a variety of normal operating and exception conditions, kept under change control throughout their life cycle, well audited, and usually supplied with additional coverage by PLCs or other similar mechanisms that ensure that ranges of acceptable values and conditions are met. They tend to have fail-safe modes that they go into whenever conditions exceed identified parameters, limit changes to certain rates, are supported by proper administrative and procedural environments that keep them operating properly, and are maintained to ensure high levels of availability. They are often in isolated or partially isolated environments and, in some cases, regulatory requirements mandate certification and accreditation processes that must be repeated when significant changes take place. Medium-surety systems are tested in all known failure modes so that their fail-safe responses can be verified; they generally have extensive acceptance tests, and changes are made only based on change orders, with the resulting changes similarly tested. Formal change and testing procedures are used, append-only media is used for auditing performance, and records are kept of every important action taken.

2.3.4.2.5 High Risks

They are (or should be) used for high-yield weapons systems, some space systems, controlling chemical plants which have highly toxic materials in close proximity to people, aircraft control systems, and other life-critical systems. The term *high risk* is usually reserved for incidents that can cause loss of life, business failure, dramatic loss in shareholder value, significant harm to the environment, significant health problems, threats to public safety, and other events that are so important they justify the extremes in effort associated with high-surety systems.

2.3.4.2.6 High Surety

High-surety systems have very specific requirements for protection that warrant physical separation, redundancy in protective barriers, special hardware designs for components, and are very expensive. High-surety systems augment the medium-surety controls with exotics. There may be multiperson controls over high-risk operations, special materials and other defensive measures may be used to create limitations on attack graphs, and passive techniques tend to be preferred to active ones.

2.3.5 Enterprise Risk Management Process: An Example

This example was the result of a development process undertaken at the request of a client for their particular situation. It has been shortened, has details removed, and has been modified to be more generic and could be reasonably applied to any enterprise with a bit of thought and effort. It consists of the following:

- Processes to be used in the overall risk management process
- Guidance on when to apply them
- A process for each of these:
  - Identifying the issues to be addressed in risk management
  - Determining when to use more in-depth processes
  - When to accept risks and not further pursue risk management
  - How to treat medium risks and what to analyze
  - How to identify consequences and how to differentiate them
  - How and when to identify threats and how to analyze them
  - How and when to do vulnerability assessments
  - Risk management choices and when to choose which of them
    - When to accept risks
    - When to transfer risks
    - When to avoid risks
    - When to mitigate risks
- Risk mitigation approaches for cases when mitigation is chosen
- Mapping of policy elements into specific risk management mandates
- A schedule for risk management, including:

  - Initial conditions required for risk management
  - Management actions required for operation
  - A schedule of activities
- How to map this risk management program into corporate reporting

2.3.5.1   The Risk Management Process

The COSO cube shows the risk management preference for Sarbanes–Oxley as identified by federal regulators. They require that risk acceptance, avoidance, mitigation, or transfer be applied by top management at all levels of the enterprise. Information protection posture assessments (IPPAs) are used to identify high risks and provide urgent, tactical, and strategic guidance for medium and low risks. These result in many instances of risks that should be accepted, transferred, avoided, or mitigated using standard techniques. Consider the following:

- After an IPPA, scenario-based and game theoretic analysis augments risk management for high consequences under medium threat.
- After an IPPA, systems analysis augments risk management for high-threat, high-consequence situations.

Explicit risk management evaluations must also be done for issues specifically identified by policy. This is done by mapping policy issues requiring risk management decisions into the risk management program.

A schedule of evaluations and process elements is built up and followed to create a regularly scheduled business process that keeps risks under proper control and adapts over time.

The risk management process is owned by the owner of the business unit or system, or by the risk management lead for the enterprise as a whole, or the chief information security officer (CISO) if nobody else is responsible for it. It is the owner's responsibility to ensure that the process is rigorously

undertaken, adequately funded, supported at all levels of management, and meaningfully applied.

2.3.5.2 Evaluation Processes to Be Used

The three evaluation processes identified for this process are IPPAs, scenario-based and game theoretic analysis, and systems analysis.

2.3.5.2.1 Information Protection Posture Assessments

This technique is based on the premise that if the proper people, processes, and support are in place, protection will be effective. It is typically cross-matched against all the different elements of a comprehensive protection program as described earlier in this chapter. Mapping to Generally Accepted Information Security Principles (GAISP), International Standards Organization (ISO) 17799, and the Capability Maturity Model for Security (CMM-SEC) are used to provide metrics for overall program performance. IPPAs are typically used as leaping-off points for determining when more in-depth analysis is required, and drill-down into any specific issue can be undertaken after the IPPA is completed. IPPAs are described in more detail at http://all.net/IPPA/index.html.

2.3.5.2.2 Scenario-Based Risk Assessment

Scenario-based risk assessment and protection evaluation is undertaken by creating sets of scenarios associated with threats, vulnerabilities, and consequences, playing strategic scenario situations out with key decision makers and experts in the fields involved, and exploring the strategic space to find reasonable approaches to mitigation. The different approaches are then codified and analyzed by game theoretic methods to find optimizations of the protective strategies. Reports are generated to determine what strategies are best aligned with the situations at hand, and decisions are made about protective measures. The scenarios are sometimes created as part of the protection posture assessment and are revisited in more detail in a scenario-based assessment to resolve the issues more clearly.

2.3.5.2.3 Systems Analysis

A model that is sometimes applied in high-risk situations is *systems analysis*. This model is limited to high-risk situations because it is expensive and time consuming and, thus, the cost of analysis becomes a significant part of the overall protective cost. This model uses a systematic and detailed analysis of all sequences of events and interactions between interdependent parts of all systems under consideration. It is not practical for detailed use in a large modern infrastructure, but, in critical infrastructure protection, the consequences may be high enough to justify its use. It is more typically used for analysis of control systems for chemical plants and similar situations in which there are limited information systems with well-defined functions controlling assets with risk to human life if these systems fail. Typically, these situations require redundant coverage of critical faults to a defined level of redundancy, extensive testing, and fail-safe systems to mitigate worst-case losses.

2.3.5.3   The Order of Analysis

Many companies do ongoing technical scans for vulnerability assessment and try to use these to sort technical countermeasures. Others start with threats and try to derive attack graphs from that starting point. The more prudent approach to strategic decision making is to start with analysis of consequences, then examine threats when the consequences warrant it, and only then look at vulnerabilities that can be attributed to the identified threats to produce the identified consequences.

2.3.5.3.1 Consequence Analysis

Consequence analysis is the first step of risk management in gaining a detailed understanding of risks. The process for developing consequences involves the following:

- Interviews are held with top management and those responsible for each system to determine the consequences associated with loss of integrity, availability, confidentiality, use control, and accountability over time.
- The expected time for detection and mitigation of loss is determined, and losses estimated if detection or mitigation fails.
- A threshold for significant loss is determined by top management. For all significant losses, further analysis is done.
- All insignificant losses are collected in a list of losses to be accepted, and management must sign off that they have decided to accept those losses should they occur.

2.3.5.3.2 Threat Analysis

After consequences are analyzed, those associated with significant losses, warranting threat analysis, are determined. Management must set a threshold for high consequences, and all other consequences worthy of consideration are treated as medium consequences. Threat analysis should involve a mix of techniques suited to the specifics of the threat environment. The mapping of these techniques into threat situations was provided earlier.

For medium-consequence items, a medium- or high-rated technique can be used. For high consequences, a high-rated technique must be used. After the initial analysis of threats by generic type, for threats identified as highly likely to have capabilities and intent to attack, techniques rated for high threats must be used. Based on these results, a threat analysis paper should be generated and updated at least yearly. Incidents within the enterprise and elsewhere in the world should inform the threat analysis process, and internal incidents should trigger investigation-based updates to the analysis.

Based on threats and consequences, top management should be provided with options to accept, avoid, transfer, or mitigate risks, and the risk management group report must identify the costs and consequences associated with each of the available options for each medium or high consequence.

2.3.5.3.3 Vulnerability Analysis

Vulnerability analysis is undertaken only when the consequences and threats are great enough to justify a detailed analysis of vulnerabilities and only after risk mitigation is identified as either a desired or viable option. At that point, a serious assessment of full-spectrum vulnerabilities should be undertaken by a qualified vulnerability assessment firm. This assessment is not the same as a penetration test or a test for known technical vulnerabilities. It should cover all aspects of protection, including but not limited to physical operations, communications, and information security and must address all paths that can induce the identified consequences. This includes collusions of multiple insiders and consequences of aggregated interdependencies.

2.3.5.4 Selection of Mitigation Approach

The key decisions in risk management are associated with the mix of risk acceptance, mitigation, transfer, and avoidance, briefly discussed as follows:

- **Risk acceptance** is the most common mode of operation today, and it results in the staggering losses we see in the marketplace. When risk management is not properly carried out, residual risk is accepted by default. When proper risk management is undertaken, residual risk is quantified and understood by the decision makers.
- **Risk transfer** typically involves insurance of some sort, but risk is indirectly transferred to shareholders when a risk is accepted.
- **Risk mitigation** typically involves the implementation of a variety of safeguards intended to reduce risk, leaving an acceptable or transferable residual risk.
- **Risk avoidance** is practiced when other alternatives are unacceptable, and usually results in not pursuing opportunities.

The form of risk mitigation to be taken can be decided by a relatively simple process. The following table provides guidance by indicating situations under which risk should be accepted without further mitigation, transferred to an insurer or some other party, reduced by protective measures, or avoided by not pursuing the business opportunity.

A more complex analysis can be done by weighting acceptability, transferability, and reducibility, and applying metrics, but instances in which such analysis is helpful are quite rare.

Acceptable	Transferable	Reducible	Action
No	No	No	Do not engage in this; avoid the risk
No	No	Yes	Propose reduction and re-evaluate
No	Yes	No	Insure or avoid the risk
No	Yes	Yes	Balance reduction with insurance cost
Yes	No	No	Accept or avoid the risk
Yes	No	Yes	Balance reduction vs. acceptance cost
Yes	Yes	No	Accept or avoid the risk
Yes	Yes	Yes	Balance all three and optimize

2.3.5.5   Specific Mitigations

The selection of specific mitigation methods is an organizational process and should be undertaken in a timely fashion to best determine specific mitigations, costs, and residual risks. The specific mitigation costs and residual risk is then balanced against risk management options to verify that mitigation is appropriate and adequate in context.

2.3.5.6   Specific Issues Mandated by Policy

Policy almost always identifies specific risk management requirements. The fulfillment of these requirements is identified in terms of what part of the policy they relate to, what the requirements are, what approach should be taken to perform the required analysis, and how often the item should be addressed. Policy mapping for this process typically takes about five days of effort for a set of policies that are systematically developed and reconciled based on a standard. If policies are not systematically developed, they should be rebuilt for proper risk management. Most often, when this is not done, there are inconsistencies, resulting in problems that require management intervention and minor policy rewrites along the way. In addition, without a consistent and properly developed policy set to drive risk management, there will most likely be uncovered areas and a lack of balance. A general requirement that risk management be applied to evaluate exceptions to policy goes across all policy areas in most enterprises.

2.3.5.7   A Schedule of Risk Management Activities

Threats and consequences have a way of changing over time. This means that risk management decisions must be revisited over time. The following table illustrates typical intervals between risk management assessments, based on threat and consequence levels. These intervals are normally based on the rate at which the consequences of change do not exceed levels management is willing to tolerate without notice. If the consequences of change are high enough to warrant management attention, then security managers need to reassess the risk, as well as the mitigation approaches they are using.

	Low Consequence	*Medium Consequence*	*High Consequence*
Low threat	Mid-level management updates annually	6-month review cycle, top-mgmt update annually	Should not occur; threats are higher
Medium threat	Mid-level management update 9–12 months	3–9-month review cycle, top-mgmt update quarterly	Continuous top-management updates monthly
High threat	Should not occur; not worth operating	3–6-month review cycle, top-mgmt update quarterly	Continuous top-management updates monthly

All substantial incidents should trigger reviews to ensure that they are within the risk management profiles set for allowable incidents and incident rates. Vulnerabilities may also be uncovered over time or induced by changes; however, if the process of risk management is properly done, changes such as these should not require reassessment, but should fall within identified tolerances. Timeframes should be based on the medium- and high-consequence columns and the medium- and high-threat rows. Other areas are not be analyzed in detail.

2.3.5.8   Initial Conditions

The risk management process depends on information and support provided to the risk management team, the following being the specific needs:

- Management must set a threshold of significant loss.
- Management must set a threshold for high loss.
- Adequate and appropriate people must work in risk management.
- Adequate funding for the risk management activity is needed.
- Organizational mandate for risk management is needed.
- Risk management information should be treated as high valued and placed in a compartment of its own.

2.3.5.9   Management's Role

Management decisions and approvals required are as follows:

- Management must agree to accept insignificant losses in writing or determine that the level of significance should be changed.
- Management must identify criteria for selection of transfer, acceptance, avoidance, and mitigation and must determine what combination of techniques should be applied to each medium- and high-consequence event identified.
- Management must allocate an adequate budget to carry out whatever risk management decision they determine to be appropriate.
- Management must oversee the risk management process and ensure that it is operating properly.

- Management must determine when changes to this process should be made and what those changes should be.

2.3.5.10   Reviews to Be Conducted

A table is built up from the set of requirements identified by policy and mandated by management with timeframes indicated by the timeframe table provided earlier. This is then turned into a schedule with timing and resourced appropriately. Contributors to the risk management program have timeframes for producing necessary materials, and their levels of effort are backed out from the risk management schedule, so they can generate their schedules and materials.

2.3.6 Threat Assessment

For effective risk management, threats may have to be assessed. Different threat assessment methodologies are suitable for different circumstances, as summarized in the following text:

- **Preemployment checks** are part of employee threat assessment. Additional investigation and review are used for positions of higher trust.
- **Case investigation** is used in response to incidents. For example, this is used if an employee gets a threatening letter that rises to the level at which the company determines that follow-up is prudent and appropriate.
- **Detailed intelligence** is undertaken against specific threats known to exist and target the company with high-valued consequences. A good example was the Irish Republican Army (IRA) bombings of financial institutions in the 1980s and 1990s. The specifics of their efforts had to be understood to counter the threat.
- **Regional intelligence** is typically used when moving into, or operating in, a region under substantial regional threat. For example, building up a business in the Middle East is clearly different from the Pacific Rim in terms of the threats faced.
- **Local intelligence** is used whenever making determinations about placement of facilities, offices, routes, or housing, and when ranking locations for determining where to go and what to do there.
- **Investigative intelligence** is typically used for clearances associated with government jobs, but it can also be used for investigation of employees for high-level-of-trust jobs, and for verification of life-style conditions such as rapid changes in wealth.

The table in the following text shows the factors in determining assessment methods. It includes the assessment method, consequence level, timeframe, threat level, and cost of assessment. As a general rule, it is better to spend less money and take less time whenever possible, but the problem with threat assessments is that until one looks into threats, one cannot determine whether they are important. As a result, it is common to do an initial threat assessment

Assessment Method	Consequence	Time	Threat	Cost
By type, generic	Medium	Short	Medium	Low
By type, classes within groups	Medium–high	Medium	Medium–high	Medium
By type with classes and detailed high relevancy	Medium–high	Medium-long	Medium–high	High
Known vulnerability indications and warnings	Medium	Short	Low	Low
Detailed intelligence analysis	High	Long	High	High
Investigation-based	Medium–high	Medium	Medium–high	Medium–high

by type at a generic level and, based on the results of this assessment and consequences associated with systems, decide on which generic threats justify more detailed investigation. Threats change over time, so periodic reassessment at the generic level is a good idea. Typically, a threat assessment is done by type at the generic level as part of a protection posture assessment and should be undertaken every few years. The next table shows a typical threat roll-up used to do a high-level summary of threats to an enterprise. This summary includes assumed values for each of 24 classes of threats, including typical funding per job, group size, motivation, skill level, hours of effort per attack process, and initial access. The table is augmented by the assessment team to indicate the level of concern and any specific concerns with respect to each threat type.

2.3.7 Fulfilling the Duties to Protect

Although it is pretty easy to create a duty to protect, fulfilling the protective duties is often quite a more difficult task. At an enterprise level, without a systematic approach to identifying, codifying, and fulfilling these duties, they are almost certain to go unfulfilled in case after case.

As a result, groups like the Software Publishers Association find companies in violation of licensing contracts and commonly gain treble damages (three times the retail value suggested by the manufacturer for every copy in use) and a right to inspect (typically, the ability to verify what software is running in every computer in the enterprise, using whatever means they see fit) for years to come. A common outcome is that they find further unlicensed software and gain more damages and rights to inspect.

One of the key factors in being able to fulfill the duty to protect is the presence of a protection architecture of the sort described elsewhere in this guidebook. With such an architecture comes a need to inventory and control information assets. With the inventory control system, it becomes feasible to identify and associate duties to protect with information and information systems. With the ability to identify and associate duties, it becomes feasible to carry out those duties.

Threat Type	Funding/Job (U.S. Dollars)	Size	Motive	Skill	Hrs/task	Access	Concern
Activists	10000	110000	Justice	Medium	10000	Insider	
Club initiates	100	350	Acceptance	Low	48	Internet	
Competitors	>100000	25	Money	Medium	2000	Industry	
Consultants	0	1	Money	Medium	No limit	Insider	
Crackers	1000–100000	1100	Malice	Medium	No limit	Internet	
Crackers for hire	>100000	110	Money	Medium	1000	Internet	
Customers	1000	15	Money	Low	1000	Partner	
Cyber gangs	<1000	1100	Money	Low	1000	Internet	
Deranged people	Usually small	1	Insanity	Any	No limit	Internet	
Drug cartels	>10M	1005000	Money/power	Medium	1000	Internet	
Economic rivals	>1B	101000	Money	High	1000	Industry	
Extortionists	100–1000	1+10	Money	Low	100	Internet	
Foreign agents and spies	>1B	>10000	Patriotism	High	No limit	Insider	
Fraudsters	100–100000	120	Money	Medium	100	Internet	
Global coalitions	>1M	10100	Money	Medium	10000	Industry	
Government agencies	>1B	>1000	Patriotism	High	No limit	Internet	
Hackers	100–10000	110	Exploration	Low	No limit	Internet	
Hoodlums	100–10000	220	Money	Low	100	Internet	
Industrial espionage experts	10000–100000	15	Money	High	1000	Industry	
Information warriors	>100M	110000	Patriotism	High	10000	Insider	
Infrastructure warriors	>1B	5100	Patriotism	High	10000	Industry	
Insiders	1000	15	Money/revenge	Medium	1000	Insider	
Maintenance people	100	15	Money	Low	10	Insider	

Military organizations	>1B	5500	Patriotism	High	10000	Industry
Nature	Unlimited	Unlimited	Randomness	Low	No limit	No limit
Organized crime	>10000	15	Money	Low	1000	Internet
Paramilitary groups	10000–100000	525	Fun/beliefs	Low	1000	Internet
Police	1000–10000	1500	Justice	Medium	No limit	Industry
Private investigators	100–10000	110	Money	Medium	100	Industry
Professional thieves	10000–100000	13	Money	Medium	1000	Industry
Reporters	1000–10000	1	Exploration	Low	100	Internet
Terrorists	10000–100000	550	Religion/power	Medium	10000	Internet
Tiger teams	15000–150000	35	Money/pride	Medium	100	Industry
Vandals	0	110	Randomness	Low	1	Internet
Vendors	1000–1000000	120	Money	High	1000	Insider
Whistle blowers		1	Justice	Low	100	Insider

Specific methods used to carry out duties to protect depend on the duties. Although relatively static approaches work for longstanding laws and regulations, a more dynamic approach is needed if a company is to deal with many complex and changing requirements. This is generally handled by the integration of an identity management approach into the implementation of the architecture in which identities are associated with all protected assets (historically called *objects*), and rules and roles are associated with human and automated actors (historically called *subjects*) in terms of the ability of the subjects to act on (sometimes called perform functions with) the objects. The roles allow grouping of subjects based on job function or similar lines, and the rules codify the rights that subjects have relative to objects. Those rights can then be translated into specific controls over specific actions within technical systems. For example, a provisioning system might configure access controls in a computer to allow a user to read a file, or elements of public key infrastructure might be provisioned to provide copies of cryptographic keys for objects to specific processes acting on behalf of specific subjects at specific times and from specific places. Similarly, audit requirements can be identified in the identity management system, and provisioning processes can be used to create audit trails associated with accesses granted over periods of time, whereas end systems and applications can provide audit trails for actions they take on behalf of actors.

2.4 Security Governance

2.4.1 Responsibilities at Organizational Levels

Responsibilities for risk management and surety levels lie with top management. Financial risk management is often carried out by a team in the CFO's office, but overall risk management may be undertaken by the audit committee, from within the chief counsel or CEO's office, or by the board of directors. IT risk management may be separated from corporate risk management and held within the CISO's office. If there is a separation between corporate and IT risk management, they need to be closely coordinated in order to be effective.

Business life cycles and deterrence are also management responsibilities. For business life cycles, business acquisition teams should include representation from the CISO function. Deterrence depends on positioning of the enterprise, decisions about when to prosecute, policy issues, and so forth. Top management also sets policy, structures protection program management, and defines the placement of information protection by positioning the CISO within the company and defining the linkage between the CISO and HR, legal, the CIO, and others.

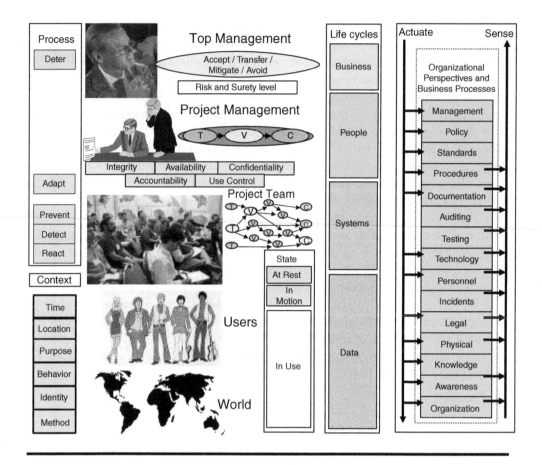

2.4.2 *Enterprise Security Management Architecture*

The overall control system that operates information protection is managed by the CISO. It typically consists of a set of increasingly detail-oriented groups that operate decreasingly sized subsets of the enterprise.

The top executives and board of directors control the functions and management associated with the CISO, regardless of the implementation of the function, its organizational location, or the management structures used to implement it. The CISO functional responsibilities include the following:

- **Business functions,** which include policies, standards, procedures, legal, HR, and risk management activities and involve the policy team, the legal department, the HR department, the risk management team, the users, and some of the project team and developers
- **Operations,** which include testing and change control, physical and informational technical safeguards, and incident handling activities, and involve the developers, systems administrators, change control team, response team, and project teams

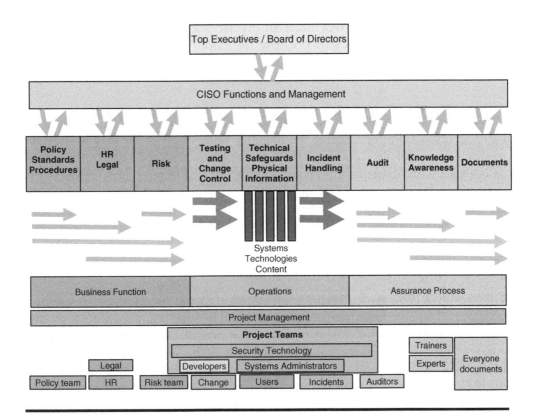

- **Assurance process,** which includes auditing processes, knowledge, and awareness programs, and documentation functions, and involves auditors, trainers, experts, project teams, everyone of course having to document what is done

Project management activities span the entire spectrum of the CISO function, although different groups of people tend to work in different areas associated with the effort. Separation of duties requirements, skill sets, organizational mandate, and other issues result in different groups operating in different parts of the organizational spectrum.

There is also a general flow of information that runs from policy, standards, and procedures through documentation, with functions on the left tending to push more information toward the functions on the right. Feedback mechanisms lead to adaptations through the control efforts associated with the CISO function.

The most critical function, the purpose of CISO, is to exert controls that influence all the different protection-related functions, listen to feedback, and make decisions that help adapt the overall enterprise protection system based on the feedback.

To carry out this function, CISO should be able to communicate effectively with top management or whoever is ultimately responsible on an enterprise-wide level for the proper operation of the business. The CISO function has to fuse together the feedback from all diverse sources, present the results to top decision makers, and explain how the controls are working or need to be changed for the protection function of the business to operate properly.

2.4.3 Groups That CISO Meets with or Creates and Chairs

CISO is responsible for assuring the ongoing value of all of the nonphysical and nonfiscal assets of the company. They manage the enterprise control system associated with information protection through groups. Those groups are generally of two sorts: (1) functional groups that perform the necessary functions for operating the protection program and (2) review board groups that review and oversee the efforts of the functional groups.

2.4.3.1   Top-Level Governance Board

The top-level governance board is an outward-facing function of the CISO. It is designed to interface between top executives, the board of directors, and other stakeholders who are responsible for overall control of the enterprise and the information protection function. This is the group that ultimately has legal responsibility for the business and its operations and determines the placement and reach of the information protection function in the enterprise. This group meets periodically with the CISO to review overall program performance and inquire about specific issues they deem worthy of their attention. Meetings should be scheduled with this group at least once per quarter and, for select functions of the CISO such as business continuity planning, additional meetings with many of the same people will also be held.

2.4.3.2   Business Unit Governance Boards

Business units that are substantial enough to operate more as wholly owned subsidiaries than as departments typically have their own internal information protection functions that fulfill some or most of their needs. Boards exist within individual business units for their internal operations and are not typically operated by the CISO function. They do have to interface with the CISO to provide enterprise-level information and ensure at the enterprise level that information protection is as it is supposed to be. The exchanges also tend to save time and money by reducing unnecessary redundancy and improving process for all.

2.4.3.3 *Policy, Standards, and Procedures Group and Review Board*

The policy, standards, and procedures group is responsible for initial policy development, reconciliation of existing policies, policy rewrites, adaptation of policy to changes in the environment, development and maintenance of control standards from policies in conjunction with the operating environment, and development of procedures associated with meeting control standards.

The review board, responsible for review and approval of policies, includes top management, making them official within the enterprise. The review and acceptance of standards by individual groups affected by those standards, approval of those standards by the proper level of management in different enterprise areas, and verifying the consistency of those standards with policies before acceptance are also controlled by this board. Individual managers are responsible for verifying that procedures meet standards and are responsible for ensuring that this is done.

Documentation of all aspects of this process must be kept. This facilitates review for new members of teams, for assurance processes to work properly, and for demonstration of regulatory compliance and other legal mandates. This should include meeting minutes, periodic plans, deliverables, progress reports, and other related documentation of the process. It should also include original data collected in the process, such as copies of e-mails associated with policy reviews, schedules for processes in whatever form the projects are tracked, ultimate dispositions of all activities, funding and costs associated with the effort, and, of course, resulting formal outputs from the process.

Project management should be used for this process and should be responsible for collecting, tracking, and reporting on all aspects of project progress, convening and scheduling meetings, and providing the CISO function with ongoing information on the overall effort.

The audit process should verify that these responsibilities are being properly carried out by selective testing of consistency by examination, verifying that the approval process is generating meaningful review prior to approval, that approval or rejection of changes is done in a timely fashion, and that policies, standards, and procedures are followed. This is done by reviewing the documentation associated with the effort, verification of proper approvals for policies, standards, and procedures in actual use, and verification of the actual operation of the overall system by selective, periodic, random, and blind review of operations against procedures, standards, and policies.

2.4.3.4   Legal Group and Review Board

The legal group varies greatly from organization to organization, depending mostly on the size and expertise of internal legal counsel. As a rule of thumb, legal review of all policies is mandatory; standards should be reviewed as well to ensure that no laws are being violated, and personnel procedures should be reviewed for issues associated with potential law suits and statutory violations. Privacy laws relating to background investigations, laws related to the specific industry, and the range of related issues associated with legal positions are particularly important in international businesses. The legal group should also be involved in incident response whenever investigatory processes are undertaken.

Legal groups generally control their own documentation and have special privileges for specific situations, so they tend to be more advisory than active participants in the protection program. Often, the CISO function has interactions with a small number of legal staff members and otherwise remains fairly independent of the legal issues except as they are used to review the work CISO is tasked with. In many cases, internal legal staff members are not experts in issues related to intellectual property law or information protection-related issues, and in these cases, outside counsel is advisable.

2.4.3.5   Personnel Security Group and Review Board

Personnel security is often coordinated by HR and carried out by a group within physical security that deals with personnel protection, facilities security, and other related issues. There is sometimes also an effort for executive protection that may be yet another group, and background checks may be performed by an outside service. This combination of activities implies that for the information protection issues to be properly covered, this activity has to be properly coordinated. HR is usually critical to the proper functioning and coordination of the functions of individuals within an enterprise, and they should almost always be the focus of these efforts. But HR also has to operate in a manner that provides the information required for effective use of protective functions such as identity management, account creation and removal, termination, leaves, medical leaves, and all other aspects of the human life cycle that imply protection changes.

Actions implied by the information protection program as well as issues related to assurance of employee rights and the proper operation of the appeals process for incidents and other matters related to employees is also in the purview of the HR department. Tracking of personnel information is an HR function that has to integrate information protection issues for coordination to take place. Clearance processes and status are HR department functions integrated with other aspects of security as well.

Documentation requirements are extensive for these processes, legal issues have to be considered, and review boards for processes as well as individual cases are required for personnel actions.

Tracking of training and awareness programs is often handled by either the HR department or a separate training group; however, tracking of educational efforts as it relates to qualifications, benefits, salary, position, and other issues is within the HR function.

The CISO has responsibility to ensure that these processes are properly undertaken and that timely and accurate information is used. This means that audit has to be involved to verify the process and that the CISO function has to coordinate the activity and influence changes necessary so that it works effectively.

2.4.3.6 Risk Management Group

The risk management group is responsible for evaluating risks and making determinations about when risk can be accepted, transferred, avoided, or mitigated. This is a core top-level business function that historically falls on top management and rightly belongs there. Unfortunately, many in top management do not clearly understand the issues of risk management when it comes to information technology, and the supporting infrastructure to provide this decision process is not in place in many enterprises. However, there is usually a risk management group that does analysis for other risk management issues, or at least a group that analyzes insurance issues and helps to determine best rates and the need for insurance.

The risk management group for information protection must invoke a process that allows top management to make rational decisions, and this is almost always a core function involving the CISO function. In fact, when there is a CISO, they are often responsible for making preliminary evaluations for all risks in this area and sole responsibility for decisions about low- and medium-risk situations. The decision to delegate risk management for these levels of risk implies a process that identifies risks and differentiates them based on consequence, and this is in the purview of the risk management group.

Risk management has to be a well-documented process in order to be meaningfully applied consistently across an enterprise. It should not depend on special expertise for day-to-day operations; however, it requires well-qualified individuals who understand how to make good judgments and understand the technology that forms the basis for the evaluations undertaken. The risk management group should tightly integrate with the CISO function.

2.4.3.7 Protection Testing and Change Control Group and Review Board

The protection testing and change control group (or groups) are responsible for measuring the effectiveness of protection on systems that warrant such controls and assuring to the desired degree of certainty that those systems operate as they are supposed to.

Results of protection testing and change controls are reviewed as a matter of course before results are accepted and systems are transitioned from testing into operational use. This is typically done by a manager responsible for the systems affected and by others who are potentially affected by the changes. For example, a change to enterprise domain name services (DNS) has to be approved by all of those responsible for medium and high risk infrastructure and systems that the DNS server supports. This serves the additional purpose of notifying all affected owners of the pending changes, and of tracking all the testing that has been undertaken to ensure that it meets the requirements of all interdependent systems.

The change control and protection testing groups must be independent of other groups because they are tasked with separating research and development from production and ensuring that errors, omissions, and acts of malice do not reach the production environment.

Protection testing is different from the sorts of vulnerability scans undertaken by common vulnerability assessment tools designed to operate in low-surety environments. These sorts of control are commonly used by systems and network administrators to detect issues they should be fixing and by auditors to verify that this maintenance work is being done. Generally speaking, systems under change control are medium- or high-surety systems in medium- or high-risk applications and, as such, they tend to be, or should be, isolated from external influences to a large extent.

2.4.3.8 Technical Safeguards Group and Review Board

The technical safeguards group is responsible for the job of risk mitigation. They apply technologies to systems to reduce the vulnerabilities of those systems and the consequences of failures in those systems.

For low-risk systems, as determined by risk management, the technical safeguards group is often left on their own in terms of protection. The CISO function typically oversees the protection of low-surety systems and seeks to make certain that they are not able to unduly influence medium- or high-surety systems through architectural methods, such as the network zoning policies, and so forth.

For medium- and high-risk systems and content, the technical safeguards team has to gain approval from risk management for mitigation approaches but takes on the primary lead for the design and implementation of technical safeguards.

They are subject to audit as well as oversight, including review by the zoning board for zone-related changes and oversight by the CISO function. Documentation is critical, legal approval has to be gained for certain potentially invasive surveillance technologies, and interface to the HR application environment is central to success of technical safeguards depending on identity management solutions. The technical safeguards team has to implement policy, help develop and follow standards, create procedures and get their approval, send changes through change control for high- and medium-surety systems, act as experts for some aspects of training and awareness, and receive education to continue to be effective in their tasks. They also have a heavy documentation burden and form part of the response capability associated with the incident handling function.

Separation of duties limits the technical team in many ways. Their central role in protection and access to so much of the potentially harmful systems places a high burden on them for reporting to others, following the rules set forth by others, and dealing with highly complex situations at high speed with strong oversight. The CISO function is typically a central aspect of this integration across the enterprise. Too many enterprises mistake the control of technical safeguards for the CISO function and miss the bigger picture.

2.4.3.9   Zoning Boards and Similar Governance Entities

Although network zoning and related matters are typically part of the technical safeguard function, there are often independent groups that review zoning policies, including system owners, network owners, risk management, audit, and incident response. Zoning boards typically include only those impacted by a change in zones or, during the creation of zones, those responsible for working within those zones.

Similar requirements may exist for classified systems and other special purpose environments that have to meet additional regulatory or jurisdictional requirements. For example, manufacturing facilities in certain industries have very specific requirements that have to be met for certain systems, and these are typically reviewed by special groups. Classified computes have special review and approval processes associated with their creation, operation, maintenance, and decommissioning. Special requirements exist for some countries, and the regulatory involvement implies participation of the legal department.

2.4.3.10   Physical Security Group and Review Board

Physical security is often handled by an independent business function with special requirements and collaboration associated with data centers, wiring, wire closets, conduits, perimeters for medium- and high-risk systems, protection of paper and other media in storage, before and after output, physical aspects of information and equipment life cycles, and integration of physical and informational access controls.

But in cases when physical security is oriented towards the facilities function rather than overall enterprise protection, or when it fails to cover all aspects of the information protection function, the CISO function has a responsibility to the enterprise to report the problem and, if a mandate is given, to manage the protection. Depending on the organization, the CISO function may have only a peripheral role in the physical security review board, may be a member of the group, or may chair the physical security group and convene the review board. In the latter case, the CISO acts more as a CSO and has broader responsibilities.

2.4.3.11   Incident Handling Group and Review Board

The incident handling group is responsible for information technology aspects of business continuity planning, disaster recovery, and day-to-day incident detection and response within the information technology function. They are, necessarily, separate from the technical safeguards team because they are tasked, among other things, with detecting trusted insider abuse. At the same time, the incident handling group is not permitted to control any of the systems, acting only through the systems administration group for low-risk systems and change control for medium- and high-risk systems to carry out any changes. This separation of duties is key to proper operation and thus the incident handling team is part of the assurance process, whereas the systems administrators, developers, and others involved in changes are part of the operations process.

The incident handling team is responsible for (1) identifying event sequences that can cause potentially serious negative consequences, (2) devising the means to detect these sequences in a timely enough fashion to mitigate harm to within enterprise-specified tolerances, (3) devising the warnings and response regimen that mitigates these consequences in the required time-frames, (4) defining the conditions under which these response processes get invoked, (5) initiating, managing, and carrying out these responses when they are required, (6) devising the process used to determine when response processes can be terminated and normal operations continued, (7) carrying out those termination processes when necessary and appropriate, and (8) after-action reports, documentation, and other related matters that produce an incident handling system that adapts properly with time.

Incident handling is often integrated with the computer security implementation team but in enterprises with medium- or high-valued systems, such as financial institutions, separation of detection from operation is very common and critically important to preventing high consequences. It is highly advisable to maintain this separation. However, some level of information flow is required for intrusion detection mechanisms to be properly tuned to the changing situation. For this reason, incident handling is part of the review process for technology changes. It serves as notice and as a means to mitigate problem technologies before they are deployed.

For low consequence systems, intrusion detection and response processes may be embedded in the systems themselves and run by systems and network administrators; however, it is useful for these systems to provide feeds to the incident handling group so they can remain aware of situations in those environments that may eventually effect them. The seeming inefficiency of separate teams may be outweighed by the larger number of incidents that have to be handled in low-surety environments and the need for higher-surety environments to be far more carefully operated and attended to. The additional duties of disaster recovery and business continuity planning also tax the incident response team for medium- and high-surety systems and may have little impact on low-consequence systems. It might be wise to use the low-surety environment for experimentation and to help train individuals who eventually move into the medium- and high-surety incident handling arena.

Incident handling includes a lot of documentation requirements, not the least of which is the collection and retention of forensic evidence associated with legal matters, and the documentation of event sequences that ultimately lead to employee sanctions and other related actions. The business continuity and disaster recovery plans have a lot of documentation as well. The interface to the legal department typically runs through a manager or perhaps the CISO for incidents of significant import. HR records get generated as a result of these actions, and the HR information associated with positions, roles, and other elements used in identity management are key to understanding and characterizing event sequences as incidents. Incident handling policies, standards, and procedures are part and parcel of the function, not only because they have to be followed, but because they have to be developed and updated. Risk management helps to decide how much incident handling effort is required for which systems, and change control provides information used in incident handling through test results that provide calibration information and configuration management that helps to determine criticality and severity of incidents.

Incident handling feeds data to auditors for evaluation of the incident handling capability and its operation and as information for audit review of the operations area. Incidents often drive awareness programs and the incident response team often acts as a provider of critical information for the awareness and knowledge requirements. Incident handling team members sometimes participate in the awareness process and are key members of the higher-level activities associated with business continuity and disaster recovery planning practice sessions.

The incident handling review board is designed to provide management with information about incidents and to get feedback on the process so as to improve it over time. Most enterprises should have quarterly reviews of incident handling and additional reviews when incidents cause substantial harm. Reviews of individual incidents should be created as part of the documentation process complete with after action reports indicative of suggested process improvements. The review board should review after-action reports prior to quarterly meetings, and summaries of these reports should be included in the overall review of the program.

2.4.3.12   *Audit Group and Review Board*

The audit group is often but not always part of the corporate internal audit function. If no such function is capable of dealing with the rigors of internal information technology audit, a separate group has to be created either within the existing enterprise organizational infrastructure or within the CISO's functional responsibility.

The audit group has a very broad range of responsibilities for reviewing and reporting on CISO functional responsibilities. This generally means that audit reports should go to the top executives or board of directors. The audits of each of the functions of the CISO should also go to the CISO so that the CISO can adapt the operation to meet the need. There is an apparent conflict of interest presented by this need to report to the CISO as part of their feedback and to report on the CISO to top management. One of the best ways to reconcile this is to have an information technology (IT) audit group that reports to the CISO and use internal audit or external audit and review processes to review the performance of the IT audit group.

IT audit has the responsibility to review the performance of every aspect of the information protection program as well as responsibility to verify that no undetected incidents take place by acting as an independent incident detection group. This implies a mix of expertise in every technical mechanism used in IT, from telephone systems to identity management infrastructure, as well as understanding of issues related to all CISO functions.

2.4.3.13   Awareness and Knowledge Group and Review Board

The awareness and knowledge group is tasked with providing a comprehensive information protection awareness program to the enterprise. This entails the collection, creation and dissemination of information appropriate to all the individuals in the company, translated into proper language and written so as to meet social norms, and presented in a manner that both conveys the important information and provides specific instructions on how to behave with regard to information protection issues relevant to the situations and tasks of the individual.

To be effective, critical awareness issues have to be repeated twice a year, and employees who have not received the awareness training and demonstrated their understanding of it have to be decertified from performing tasks until they come into compliance. This implies a system of tracking all users and their currency in security training and awareness for all tasks they are assigned to perform. As changes in responsibility occur, training and awareness have to be updated.

In addition to all the tracking of program execution and compliance, the awareness program has to be updated on a regular basis, so that it does not become stale. A variety of techniques are available and should be rotated and applied over time to keep interest levels high. The program should produce well-documented results that can be readily reviewed on an annual basis to ensure that the program is operating properly. This review is typically done by the CISO as part of their normal processes. Legal review and long-term documentation should be retained to mitigate any disputes for the duration of the applicability of the training material or its historical value.

2.4.3.14   Documentation Group

The documentation of information protection tends to be extensive and involves many different people. Typically, there is a corporate documentation standard, an archival function and document repository, a tracking process that includes aging and life-cycle management for destruction processes, and a set of retention policies, standards, and procedures that support this function. A library system is often used to track all this information, including the requirement to categorize and retrieve data, librarians, and off-site backup storage of important documents. This system should track the whole documentation produced through the CISO function and provide easy retrieval and access for authorized individuals, including the CISO and all members of the review boards, relative to the material they review. This group should also provide the means for audit and other related functions to gain access to materials, and provide historical data and research capabilities.

Documentation is often systematically produced through the use of professional project managers as part of the project management process. It is helpful for the CISO to maintain a project management process surrounding all efforts both to track everything and to provide clear documentation of processes and outcomes. Documentation has to have proper classification and applicability to ensure that it is properly protected within the enterprise protection architecture.

2.4.4 Issues Relating to Separation of Duties

Separation of duties is a key issue in information protection, but at the CISO level, management has to coordinate all aspects of the protection program for it to be effective. What really has to be separated is not management of the overall information protection program, but the implementation of controls. Different checks and balances exist for management than for implementation. In effect, the audit process covers management issues, whereas management covers the separation of duties for CISO functions.

2.4.5 Understanding and Applying Power and Influence

Power produces influence and different forms of power are used to influence different people and groups in different ways.

2.4.5.1   Physical Power

Because of physical security mechanisms and guard forces, physical security can be a means of exerting power. Having physical access to information systems and infrastructure, being able to lock offices or lock people out of facilities, and the use of guards to escort individuals to termination meetings are examples of how physical power can be used to influence outcomes. Physical force tends

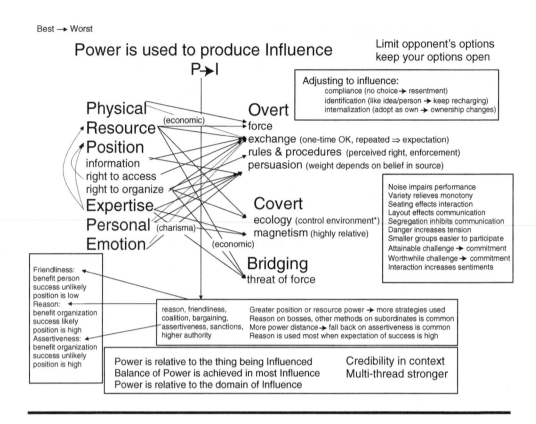

Best → Worst

Power is used to produce Influence
P→I

Limit opponent's options
keep your options open

Physical
(economic)

Resource

Position
information
right to access
right to organize

Expertise

Personal (charisma)

Emotion (economic)

Overt
force
exchange (one-time OK, repeated ⇒ expectation)
rules & procedures (perceived right, enforcement)
persuasion (weight depends on belief in source)

Covert
ecology (control environment*)
magnetism (highly relative)

Bridging
threat of force

Adjusting to influence:
compliance (no choice → resentment)
identification (like idea/person → keep recharging)
internalization (adopt as own → ownership changes)

Noise impairs performance
Variety relieves monotony
Seating effects interaction
Layout effects communication
Segregation inhibits communication
Danger increases tension
Smaller groups easier to participate
Attainable challenge → commitment
Worthwhile challenge → commitment
Interaction increases sentiments

Friendliness:
benefit person
success unlikely
position is low
Reason:
benefit organization
success likely
position is high
Assertiveness:
benefit organization
success unlikely
position is high

reason, friendliness,
coalition, bargaining,
assertiveness, sanctions,
higher authority

Greater position or resource power → more strategies used
Reason on bosses, other methods on subordinates is common
More power distance → fall back on assertiveness is common
Reason is used most when expectation of success is high

Power is relative to the thing being Influenced
Balance of Power is achieved in most Influence
Power is relative to the domain of Influence

Credibility in context
Multi-thread stronger

---

to be overt and direct, although some level of indirectness can be used to imply
a physical threat. But this is often considered undesirable in the context of an
enterprise and should only be used when necessary for the situation. For
example, physical escort is normally used when an employee is terminated, as
disputes often arise in this context. Physical power almost always produces
compliance in enterprises rather than identification or internalization.

2.4.5.2   Resource Power

Resources can come in many forms, typically, from things that can be
exchanged, such as money, facilities control (space), people (time), computing
resources, network resources, control over the environment (ecology), and
the threat of force. Overt resource power tends to produce compliance and,
in some cases, identification. If the resource power is directed toward something that is already desirable to the target of the influence, identification and
internalization can both be achieved, but usually only as long as the resource
continues to be made available.

2.4.5.3   Positional Power

Positional power stems from three aspects: access to information, the ability
to grant access, and the right to organize. Information can be used for its

exchange value or as a tool of persuasion. For example, it is sometimes used as leverage by allowing its use without disclosure or is sometimes concealed to create an elite class with the power to apply it.

- The ability to grant access can be used for exchanges; however, if done repeatedly, it creates an expectation of trading value that may be undesirable.
- Information and access rights are effective at producing compliance when that information forces an unpopular move, but more often it leads to identification in small quantities and internalization when it is particularly useful.
- The right to organize is typified by work roles, assignments, titles, pay levels, and so forth. It tends to lead to compliance at best when it is a demotion, but when used for advancement or restructuring with positive attributes, it leads to internalization or identification.

Positional power in the information protection arena is often exercised through the use of matrix management, project teams, reassignment of people to teams under the CISO, or other similar steps. But this influences other issues such as budgets, organization sizes, and so forth, and all these have impacts on how people think of themselves and the relative importance of managers. As a result, positional power has management interactions that can be touchy from a political standpoint and influence apparent financial results of organizations. As a simple example, if security is a cost center that is handled by the business unit but can be moved into the CISO's office and be handled as a cost by the enterprise, it reduces the apparent costs to profit centers so that individual business units can claim higher margins, even though they may not have changed anything but the structure of the enterprise. These results may be tied to performance bonuses or other metrics that benefit individuals.

2.4.5.4 *Expertise, Personal, and Emotional Power*

Expertise can be used for persuasion, magnetism, and as a threat of force. For persuasion, the weight of influence depends on the belief of the audience in the source. Magnetism is highly relative and, with few exceptions, is ineffective at high levels in the enterprise environment. The threat of force associated with expertise is based on the notion that the expertise can be used against others, but this is an oppositional perspective only really used in the context of questioning suspects and similar interview processes. Personal persuasion is based on a trust relationship that goes to liking and is commonly used in the enterprise as a way to leverage relationships for benefits. Emotional persuasion and exchange involves elicitation techniques. In the context of information protection, building up personal relationships is always a benefit in working through complex issues, and it provides a great deal of access and information of great value.

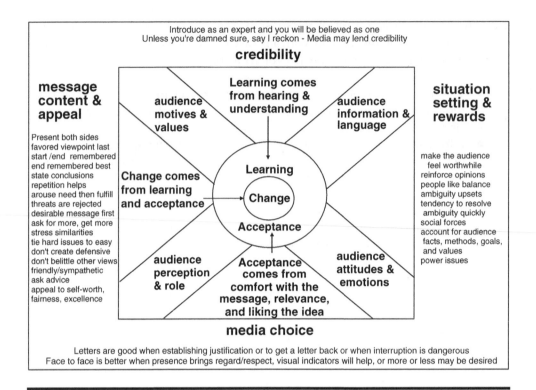

2.4.5.5   Persuasion Model

When persuasion is key, as in most situations encountered by CISOs, there is a well-known persuasion model that helps understand these issues and address them systematically. This model is credited to Chester L. Karrass who is famous for his graduate work and subsequent courses on negotiations. The basic principle of persuasion is that change comes from the learning and acceptance of the goal viewpoints. Learning comes from perceiving the message and understanding it. Acceptance comes from comfort with the message; it must be relevant, and the person being persuaded must like the idea. This implies a certain understanding of the audience. Specifically, audience motives and value, information and language, perception and role, and attitudes and emotions lead to selection of techniques for persuasion.

- **Message content and appeal:** Studies have shown that persuasion is more effective if both sides are presented with the favored viewpoint presented last. The start and end of a presentation are better remembered, with the end remembered best. Conclusions should be clearly stated, and repetition helps, as with the formulaic approach of saying what you are going to say, saying it, and saying what you have said. It helps to arouse a need and then fulfill it. Threats tend to be rejected, and it is better to put the desirable message first. In negotiations, the more you ask for, the more you get. It is better to ask for everything and only back off slowly in exchange for large concessions. It is better to stress similar points of view and reduce disagreements without belittling other views. Tying hard issues to easy ones sometimes help to solve the hard ones. Being friendly and sympathetic helps, and asking advice on how to resolve problems without sacrificing enterprise needs often generates a cooperative environment. Avoid creating defensive situations to prevent hardening views. Appeals to excellence, self-worth, and fairness work.

- **Situation, setting and rewards:** Setting is important to delivery of the message. Try to make the audience feel worthwhile and to reinforce their opinions. People like balance, but ambiguity upsets them and there is a tendency to resolve ambiguity quickly. Balance should be presented without unnecessary production of lingering ambiguity. If a problem is created, it should be readily resolved by agreeing with the presenter's view. Social forces should be considered and the audience point of view must be accounted for. Facts, methods, goals, and values are used to influence decisions, and power issues are always relevant.
- **Credibility:** If introduced as an expert, the presenter will be seen as one. Media, presentation, clothing, degrees, experience, and references tend to increase credibility. Avoid opinions on issues you do not know much about to retain credibility, particularly among experts.
- **Choice of media:** Letters are good when establishing justification, when it is desired to get a letter back, or when interruption is dangerous. A face-to-face discussion is better when presence brings regard or respect, when visual indicators help guide direction, or when more or less may be desired.

2.4.5.6   Managing Change

Changes are always met with resistance. It is the nature of things. Managing change is fundamental to making the changes associated with information protection programs over time. The greater the change, the more resistance you are likely to encounter. When change is introduced you will hear, "You must be crazy" and similar phrases. As people experience change, they will express disbelief. Eventually, they will embrace the change if they believe it benefits them, and you will hear remarks such as "No way! Really!!" As the new becomes the norm, the doubters will brag that they were with you all the way and that they knew it all along. Such is life.

The success of the change plan depends on the way expectations are managed. The basic plan is to understand what will be different, who it will affect, how to prepare those affected, how the change plan could fail, and how to treat the things that could cause it to fail before they do so. The effort in planning change involves the creation of a buy-in plan, a communications plan, and a set of risk treatment plans. And, of course, it must be understood that no plan survives contact with the enemy.

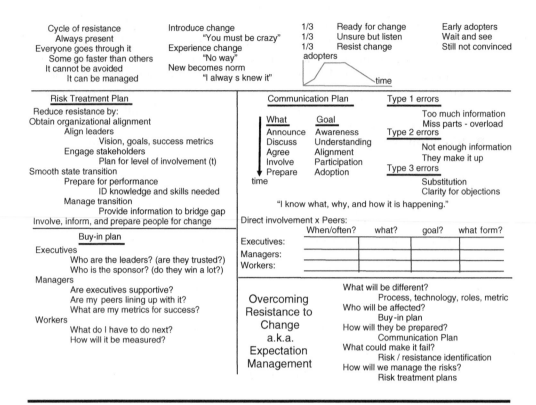

2.4.5.6.1 The Buy-In Plan

Executives and leaders in nonhierarchical structures need to know who is leading the efforts for change and must build up trust in those leaders to buy into the plan. This often means finding a champion at the executive level in the right organization to help sponsor the effort. Although some CISOs have direct access to and the trust of top management, others are forced to create alliances for change with those above them in the structure. The sponsors of the effort for change are typically top-level executives who, for one reason or another, decide it is in their or the company's best interest to make the changes indicated. The higher they are, the better the chances of success.

Managers and other facilitators have to gain executive support to see the benefits in helping changes happen. Whereas many security changes are started with workers and grow "organically," managers who champion change ultimately need executive support to make large-scale changes. Managers also have to line up support with their peers to make changes, and this is often a complex process, involving a lot of leadership and time. Finally, managers have to find ways for their efforts for change to be reflected in the metrics used to measure their success in the organization, or they will be punished for their efforts. If executive management cannot be persuaded to create metrics that support managers making these changes, the program cannot succeed.

Workers predominantly need to know what they have to do next and how their performance in those tasks will be measured to buy into the effort. Their cooperation is vital to success, and they need to have sets of rewards and punishments in order to willfully join in the effort to change.

2.4.5.6.2 The Communications Plan

Over time, the CISO will announce subjects for awareness to target audiences, discuss these with the audiences to develop mutual understanding, come to agreement so that people are aligned to the change, involve the targets to gain their willing participation, and prepare the targets so that they can successfully adopt the changes. Your goal should be that the targets of your efforts would say, "I know what is changing, why it is changing, and how it is happening."

The targets of your effort depend on the structure of the organization. For hierarchies, they typically include executives, managers, and workers that are directly and indirectly affected by the changes. For network organizations, replace executives by key influential people and work down the influence hierarchy corresponding with managers and workers, providing all affected individuals with the information they need to understand, from their point of view: what is changing, why it is changing, and how the change will happen. The communications plan should specifically codify when and how often each target audience should be communicated with and by whom, what is to be communicated with them, and toward what objective (what, why, or how of the change); the form of the communication should be selected to meet the need according to the persuasion model.

The communications plan should seek to avoid errors of omission (type 1), errors of commission (type 2), and errors of substitution (type 3). Errors of omission come when too much information is provided, leading to cognitive overload which causes important points to be missed. Errors of commission occur when not enough information is provided, resulting in people making up their own versions of what, why, and how. Errors of substitution happen when inadequate clarity is present to overcome mental objections and predispositions toward other answers to what, why, and how.

2.4.5.6.3 The Risk Treatment Plans

The risk to change stems from the combination of natural resistance as described earlier, vested interests such as ownership of the previous approach, and real reasons associated with risk management and other performance metrics of the enterprise. If these objections cannot be rationally overcome and influence approaches are ineffective, the road to change will be very hard indeed.

The process by which project-related risk of completion is treated is typically very different from the risk processes associated with computer security-related risks, and this difference must be clearly understood. Organizational risks are mitigated by alignment of human forces and creating smooth transitions that do not unduly disrupt the normal course of business or create unnecessary friction.

Typically, organizational alignment starts with aligning the leadership around vision, goals, and metrics for success. Once the leaders agree on these factors, stakeholders have to be engaged. It is usually a good idea to start engaging the stakeholders long before leadership makes a commitment, because leadership will ask stakeholders about these issues, and if the stakeholders they ask do not buy into the program, the risk of failure will increase substantially. It is usually a good idea to have a plan for involving stakeholders in various processes associated with the change as a function of the process. This means getting their initial and ongoing support and continuing to keep them informed and involved at the appropriate level. In some cases, this means finding ways to get stakeholders who disagree with the change not to disrupt the process, and this can be complex as well. For example, in some cases, effective change is attained by getting disruptive stakeholders to engage in other activities that make them too busy to interfere with the change. In other cases, marginalizing their views to key group members or finding ways to give them something they want in exchange for cooperation works. Although this may seem complicated, underhanded, and unnecessary to the typical technical expert who has been moved into a management position, it is commonplace among managers and executives who have to find ways to get the system to support their, often competing, ends.

Smooth transition is desirable but not always attainable. The goal is to minimize friction, and this is done by preparing people for what they will have to do and managing the transition from the previous operation to the subsequent one. To prepare for performance, it is important to identify the specific information, skills, and knowledge needed by each of the different sorts of individuals involved. To manage the transition more smoothly, information has to be provided to bridge the gap between the previous and subsequent states. In other words, the idea is to involve, inform, and prepare people for change.

2.4.5.6.4 Adaptation to Contact

Of course, all the planning for change will not prevent resistance and that resistance may come in any number of forms. To prevent change, many people may push back against the change by using their influence and power, they may refuse to cooperate by withholding information, or they may try to use any of the other aspects of power discussed in the power and influence section of this guidebook. Although risk treatment plans can cover many of these issues, there will always be some that are missing. Do not panic. Learn ways to counter verbal and nonverbal attacks by studying the subject matter in more detail. Practice the methods outlined here and try to understand what underlies the resistance, so you can turn it away or build bridges that help you overcome it.

2.4.5.6.5 Managing Security Consulting Jobs: An Example

One of the best examples of resistance to change comes when IPPAs are done for the first time in an organization. By the nature of an IPPA, there has to be an internal sponsor and an external assessment team. If the internal sponsor does not properly prepare the field, the external team will meet with great resistance, but ultimately it is the job of the external team to help the internal sponsors do their job. The assessment team leader has a customer relationship and expectation management problem every time, but in this case, it is at an extra level of indirection because the assessment team manager has to get the internal sponsor to manage the internal politics. There are two basic problem cases, both of which occurred during a recent assessment: someone with inadequate skills, power, and influence as the insider, or an insider who is so powerful that the individual creates powerful resistance.

In this recent assessment, the sponsor of the effort was the CEO of the enterprise. This is a very good situation in the sense that nobody is more likely to be empowered to get the job done than someone who comes at the request of the CEO. But on the other hand, the members of the executive team felt a bit put upon by the mandate from above to review their parts of the enterprise. So the resistance came from the top-level executive team members. In the meanwhile, one of those team members was told by the CEO to identify an appropriate person to coordinate the IPPA, and that team member chose someone who had essentially no power or influence but a great deal of technical expertise to run the effort. So the full force of the CEO was theoretically available but the CEO was unavailable to use any of that power to actually help get the job done, creating the most powerful possible set of resistance and the least powerful internal lead.

The assessment itself had many problems, including people who refused to attend meetings or missed scheduled meetings, people who told their employees not to be helpful and tried to mislead the assessment team, and people who instructed protective forces to act in very abnormal ways so that they could keep the assessment team from finding any flaws; the list goes on and on. Eventually, a draft assessment report was provided that indirectly indicated the need for a powerful lead for information protection without unduly offending the internal assessment lead who was the first reviewer. Over the assessment team leader's objections, the document was sent to too many people in its draft form, eventually leading to a great number of complaints about factual errors in parts of the draft report that had not been vetted yet.

When a private meeting with the CIO was requested to review the draft report and its findings, the CIO agreed but then set up a meeting with all of the leads responsible within the CIO organization and tried to get the assessment team leads to come to that meeting. It was explained to the CIO that this was the part in which we interviewed her and not the one in which her team was supposed to be present. We indicated that many of the subjects we were going to discuss were what she might not want to share with her team, such as their performance in various areas from her perspective and staffing-level issues. The meeting was held with the CIO alone, and lasted for several hours, much of which was spent discussing matters she should have been informed about through an effective communications plan but was not because the internal lead did not have the necessary access to the CIO to get the job done.

The CIO seemed to start accepting the process after this meeting, but the resistance was not yet over. A copy of the current draft report was sent to the CIO that evening as she prepared for an executive committee and board meeting the following day. She had decided that she was being treated unfairly by the process and was determined to discredit the report before anyone else had a chance to read it. Of course, the report was still a draft because she had not had the opportunity to make her comments on it. She was still unhappy about many of its features because someone else within the organization had prepared her for its alleged negative bias against her. Actually, it said nothing about her because she had not yet been interviewed. The study lead got wind of the situation through other internal sources close to the CEO, and the CEO was prepared for any conflict based on the notion that the report was still a draft and that with her cooperation, the CIO could help to form the report into a helpful internal document. She could not really argue the point.

Several weeks later, the CIO requested an additional meeting to discuss the draft report in more detail. This meeting started at 4 P.M. at her office and went on till about 9 P.M. In this meeting, the assessment lead spent time one-on-one with the CIO discussing many of the issues in the report. It was clarified that just because many potential vulnerabilities were found, it did not mean that they all needed to be fixed. The risk management process was better explained as a process of executive decision making and not a process in which executives are forced to spend budget on things they do not want. Some disputes from a key manager about findings were reviewed, and the assessment lead indicated that the individual had put up substantial resistance, forcing the team to check the facts out very carefully. The lead indicated that he personally saw the records, checked the facts, and that the manager had tried to avoid the process and prevent the information from being made available. This was indicated as a management problem that the CIO needed to address. The top priorities for fixing critical issues were discussed at length and the CIO came to agree that the identified items really did need to be fixed and that nothing identified as having to be done was unreasonable or inappropriate. Cost and internal political issues were discussed at length and considerable clarity was achieved.

About two months later, a verbal report and presentation was made to the executive committee regarding this assessment and a series of related assessments under way. When the IPPA was discussed and the results reviewed, the assessment team lead was prepared for further resistance, but none came. The CIO indicated to the executive committee that five of the seven key recommendations were either already completed or were being implemented.

The remaining recommendations were long-term and would likely be undertaken in the appropriate timeframes.

It should be clear that this was not the ideal situation and that the key elements of the change process could not be handled by the internal assignee. But despite the problems along the way, the change was made, and it eventually came to be embraced. Learning to manage change is the key to the CISO's success.

2.4.6 *Organizational Perspectives*

From an organizational perspective, the program involves a broad range of activities and contexts. Issues arise in these different contexts. Although more in-depth information on each of these areas is necessary to carry out the more detailed work associated with them, from a CISO point of view, these details need to be covered at the next level of management. Results are analyzed and rolled up into reports included as part of the feedback process. The underlying issues that should be addressed are identified in more detail in the following subsections.

2.4.6.1 *Management*

Management is typically handled by the CISO, who helps to build management practices and coordinates management of information protection throughout the enterprise. It includes the following:

- **People** who have to be trained, made aware, tracked, and managed.
- **Budgets** that have to be generated, justified, and used wisely.
- **Effects** created by actuators that allow the CISO and others to influence events that take place.
- **Sensor** outputs from sensors including automation, people, and groups, reported to the CISO for situation awareness.
- **Controls** formed from sensors and actuators. As a feedback system, the CISO uses technologies, procedures, processes, and other things within direct and indirect power and influence to control the process.
- **Planning** required to cause the complex event sequences involving people and systems to be properly coordinated.
- **Strategy** that translates the long-term vision of the enterprise and the CISO into the plans that result in achieving those long-term goals.
- **Tactics** that provide the short-term event sequences that produce the functional behaviors desired in specific situations.
- **Coordination** that assures that the tactics as implemented remain within the desired set of future sequences.
- **Politics** that form the basis of the interactions between people throughout the enterprise and, if successfully applied, allow the CISO to control the situation without creating unnecessary friction.

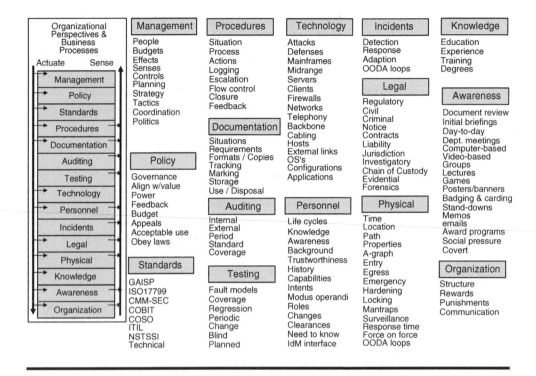

2.4.6.2   Policy

Policy codifies the intent of the enterprise starting at the top level.

- **Governance** implies the system under which power and influence operate. These are the processes that take place within the enterprise, its institutions, and its structures to allow those in charge to govern.
- **Alignment with value** indicates the policy need to tie value to the enterprise to the time, effort, and cost associated with protective functions.
- **Power** issues are codified in policy by granting individuals and groups control over resources, actions, titles, and other influential items.
- **Feedback** issues provide the means by which policy may be used to close the control loop at the top level of the enterprise.
- **Budget** and the process by which policy dictates that budget is generated and managed provides the means of controlling critical fungible resources.
- **Appeals** processes define the manner in which policies and decisions made by those granted power and influence under policy may be challenged.
- **Acceptable use** identifies what is and is not acceptable in the use of corporate resources.
- **Obeying laws** is typically codified in policy to ensure that employees do not go astray under the corporate banner and provides the necessary mandate to provide the necessary knowledge to employees to prevent ignorance as an attempted excuse.

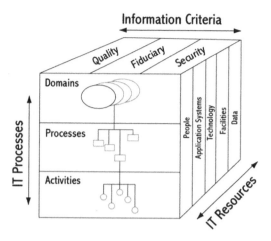

2.4.6.3   Standards

Standards include specific enterprise control standards that codify policy in more detail and, at the CISO's level, commonly accepted and practiced approaches to information protection that codify due diligence and reasonable and prudent approaches.

- The Generally Accepted Information Security Principles (**GAISP**) have evolved from Generally Accepted System Security Principles (**GASSP**). These principles are fundamental top-level issues that are key to effective information protection and should be codified as appropriate in every information protection program. They were developed by a committee within the Information Systems Security Association (ISSA), a not-for-profit international organization of professionals and practitioners. (http://www.issa.org/gaisp/gaisp.html) The primary goal of the ISSA is to promote management practices that ensure confidentiality, integrity, and availability of information resources.
- **ISO17799-2005** is the International Standards Organization's adaptation of British Standard BS7799 and updated from ISO17799. It defines issues at one level deeper than GAISP and codifies the most common issues identified by companies in their implementation of information protection. It is designed so that management has the option of determining what to do and to what extent it should be done. Audits against ISO17799 generally adopt the notion that all the elements must be done to a reasonable and prudent extent based on the situation in the enterprise.
- **CMM-SEC** is the capability maturity model security interpretation. It codifies the maturity level of a security engineering capability, but it is very useful as a management tool because it largely codifies these capabilities from a standpoint of how effectively they are managed. The CMM-SEC is not a formal standard. However, it is the best codification of these issues available and has utility for the CISO.

- **CoBit** (see the CoBit Cube) was developed as a generally applicable and accepted standard for good IT security and control practices. It provides a reference framework for users, management, and IT audit, control, and security practitioners. CoBit is sponsored by the Information Systems Audit and Control Association (ISACA) with its Web site at http://www.isaca.org/.
- **COSO** is the risk management standard created by the Committee Of Sponsoring Organizations of the Treadway Commission. COSO is the preferred regulatory framework for Sarbanes–Oxley section 404 (SOX 404) risk management as specified by the regulators in the United States. As such it is mandatory and applies to all public companies in the United States. COSO is also widely accepted around the world. The COSO cube gives an overview of COSO. SOX 404 and COSO say nothing about information technology.

- **The Information Technology Infrastructure Library (ITIL)** provides a "cohesive set of best practice" to implement British Standard Institute (BSI) standard for service management (BS15000). It includes a guide on implementing security in service level agreements (SLAs).
- **The National Security Telecommunications System Security Initiative (NSTSSI)** provides a set of national standards (numbers 4011 and higher) for training personnel who have responsibility for creating, operating, approving, and overseeing secure systems. This includes information security professionals, systems administrators, system certifiers, and designated approving authorities. These standards are available for review at http://all.net/books/standards/NSP/index.html.
- **Technical standards** exist for many different aspects of information protection and, as a rule of thumb, it is better to go with standards-based solutions than nonstandard solutions because of the complexity of interfacing nonstandard systems and capabilities to other systems and capabilities.

- Enterprises also have and develop **control standards** that codify policies so as to provide additional and more detailed guidance for implementation. These control standards act as a bridge between policies and procedures by providing specifics on how to implement policy without delving into the details of systems.

This toolkit is a standards-based approach to information protection and, as such, following it will help ensure compliance with standards and good outcomes in audits, as well as reasonableness, prudence, and diligence of practices.

2.4.6.4 Procedures

Procedures implement standards in specific systems and contexts by creating systematic step-by-step processes that, if properly followed, result in meeting those standards. Procedures codify the processes at the lowest level of implementation and, typically, generate documentation associated with each of the following steps:

- **Situation** leads to process. As a result, most procedures have sets of preconditions for their invocation. They can, in many cases, be codified in a production system that identifies the conditions and triggers the actions associated with that condition.
- **Process** is carried out through situation-specific actions that get logged, escalation conditions, control over process flows, feedback loops within and outside each process to ensure quality, and termination conditions that cause processes to end and be formally closed out.
- **Actions** associated with procedures are typically designed to result in some set of specific outcomes.
- **Logging** is undertaken to ensure that a record is made of what took place and to allow after-action analysis and reporting for process evaluation and improvement. Logging processes also produce the documentation necessary for legal and other review purposes.
- **Escalation** is typically the result of an exception that is codified as part of overarching procedures to ensure continued process control even when the process gets out of the predefined control scheme.
- **Flow control** mechanisms typically ensure that work is performed in order and that results are checked along the way. Approval processes may also be involved. These are often implemented in ticketing systems or similar control mechanisms. Some flows allow limited parallelism.
- **Closure** is the result of the process reaching a conclusion. Ticketing systems or similar systems indicate that no further work is pending on the process.
- **Feedback** occurs at all levels, from the process components that lead to situational changes dictating further actions to the overall feedback that improves processes by after-action reports and other more strategic reviews.

2.4.6.5   Documentation

Documentation is created throughout the overall information protection process, creating a need to capture and protect that documentation and to use it for investigation, analysis, and other legal and business purposes.

- **Situations** dictate the need for documentation of different sorts. Although novel situations may require unique documentation, most situations are recurrent. As they recur, the documentation processes and formats become standardized.
- **Requirements** documents are used to describe what is required for systems when implemented. There are typically specific documentation requirements for different purposes, and those requirements are themselves documented to formalize the documentation process.
- **Formats** associated with documents become standardized as the situations leading to them recur. These formats lead to implementation in databases for more systematic analysis and process improvement. Formats also apply to marking and tracking processes.
- **Copies** may be made of documentation. This is beneficial for availability but potentially harmful for confidentiality and may be legally restricted.
- **Tracking** takes place at many levels. Documents of certain sorts, such as limited access documents, protected health information, financial records of certain sorts, trade secrets, and classified documents must be tracked throughout their life cycle and the tracking itself is a form of documentation. Large-scale document tracking systems are also vital to retaining and searching large numbers of corporate records, ensuring that other processes are carried out at the proper time, and being able to demonstrate that the document control process is operating properly.
- **Marking** is commonly used to allow inspection to identify document types and control information. Markings are required for certain documents, including documents with intellectual property value. Marking is also the basis for much of the automated and manual process associated with document control.
- **Storage** becomes complex and problematic for large numbers of documents, especially, mixed combinations of paper, fiche, other physical media, and electronic documents that are interrelated. Tracking systems are helpful in locating and retrieving stored documents as well as determining when storage must be refreshed. Storage also involves environmental controls that are specific to specific media.
- **Use** of documents involves a variety of control issues, including access control, application control, protection from corruption, continued availability, treatment of drafts, and so forth.
- **Disposal** is another key issue in information protection and document disposal is particularly problematic for many enterprises. The failure to properly dispose of waste is one of the most common faults detected in penetration tests, and the results are sometimes dramatic. Documenting disposal of documents is also important as are assurances associated with retention requirements as they relate to disposal.

2.4.6.6 Auditing

Auditing provides the means for management to verify the proper operation of the information protection program.

- **Internal audit** processes ensure that operations meet internal requirements on a day-to-day basis. This typically involves a substantial number of audit staff and a cyclical process that ensures that high-valued systems are revisited often, whereas lower valued systems are covered consistent with their value.
- **External audit** processes act as independent verifications that operations are as they are supposed to be and also act to ensure that internal audit is effectively doing its job.
- **Periodicity** for audits is a nontrivial matter with audit periods determined by risks, costs, resources, and time and cost to audit. Random audits, surprise audits, regular audits, and other time-related issues fall under this broad category.
- **Standards** are typically what audits compare realities to. Auditors are generally tasked with relating performance to a standard so that a consistent basis for opinions can be used and comparisons can be done over time and between systems and organizations. It is normal to use the same standards for protection as are used for audit so that the audit provides reconcilable feedback on the adequacy of the program in meeting the standards set for it.
- **Coverage** expresses the extent to which audit processes cover the set of subjects that could possibly be checked in an audit. It acts as a metric on the audit itself as well as a means to evaluate the value of the audit. An audit that is passed but only covers an unimportant subset of the issues or systems at hand is not a very good reflection of the situation and has little utility.

2.4.6.7 Testing and Change Control

Protection testing provides verification that protection does what it is supposed to do. It involves the following issues:

- **Fault models** are basic phenomenological models of the sorts of faults that occur and how they are manifested to the observer.
- **Coverage** is expressed as a numerical value indicating the percentage of the whole event sequences covered by the testing regimen relative to the fault model.
- **Regression** testing requires that tests against historical weaknesses are done to verify that events that used to be problems do not recur.
- **Periodic** testing requires that the enterprise define periods between tests based on system factors like criticality, rate of change, complexity, and so forth.
- **Change** generates a requirement for regression testing and new test development associated with the changed functionality. Levels of change

that require testing must be defined based on the criticality of the systems under test and the nature of the changes. This integrates with the change management system to form a systematic change control process. A sound change control process is preferred for medium-risk systems and mandatory for high-risk systems. Sound change control requires the following:

- All changes are based on requirements specified and approved by people who are not involved in making the change.
- Changes must be provided in source code and executable form to the change control process.
- The change control process may not alter the provided code.
- The change control process must read the code involved. The code must be straight forward, easily understood, and clearly address the specific change requirement.
- The code must make no unnecessary or unrelated changes.
- Change control must go through a well-defined testing process after the changed code is manually and automatically analyzed.
- After independent compilation within change control, verification must be undertaken to ensure that the binary images match.
- After suitable management and technical approvals, only unaltered original information provided to change control is put into production.
- **Blind testing** is used such that the individuals operating the system under test are unaware that a test is under way. A methodology for carrying out such tests is required.
- **Planned tests** also need well-defined circumstances and performance requirements.

2.4.6.8   *Technical Safeguards: Information Technology*

Risk mitigation often involves technologies. Implementing and operating those technologies requires significant effort and expertise.

- **Attacks** are typically codified as sequences of events carried out by a threat. Attack processes are described elsewhere in this book.
- **Defenses** are measures that act to (1) reduce threats, (2) reduce the ability of threats to find and exploit vulnerabilities, (3) reduce the number of vulnerabilities and control their nature, type, and location, (4) reduce the linkage between exploitations of vulnerabilities and consequences, and (5) reduce consequences.
- Different technical safeguards apply to different **environments**. As a rule of thumb, at least the following sets of environments have to be considered for technical safeguards:
- **Mainframes** typically have access controls based on user identity involving a subject/object model. They are centrally controlled for large application environment with sound change control over program changes, strong and standardized audit components, and limited user interfaces. They may also house database systems that have query limits. They often have redundant system capabilities, and they tend to use separation of duties.

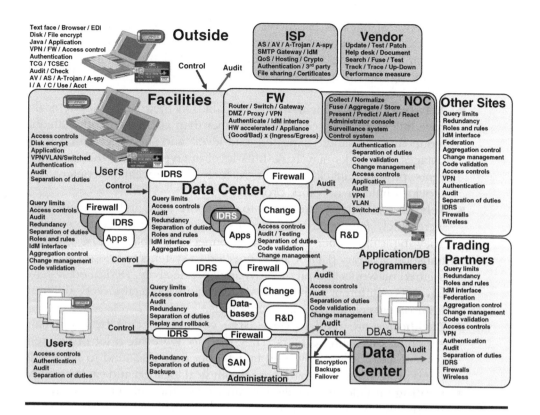

- **Midrange** computers typically handle local operations, control production, distribution, or other specialized systems, and have protection similar to those of mainframes, but on a smaller scale.
- **Servers** may be mainframes, midrange computers, or other types of devices but, increasingly, they are run on small system platforms with Linux, Unix, or Windows operating systems. They have protection associated with the operating systems. Many have power and disk redundancy, audit controls, and query limits. Some use separation of duties and are change-controlled, most have access control in one form or another, and many interact with identity management infrastructure for access control. Applications in those servers may have additional controls.
- **Clients** are typically single-user systems, usually run a low-surety operating system, and usually have minimum controls. They form the largest set of platforms, tend to be vulnerable, are often poorly managed, and are subject to all sorts of attacks, ranging from viruses and worms to Trojan horses. Thin client platforms that have strong controls are less expensive alternatives, but they tend to be less popular today.
- **Firewalls** are typical network separation devices and may be implemented as "firewall routers," as separate components in a perimeter architecture, as software components in end systems, or as separation devices between enclaves or network zones. Firewalls generally have a network interface control capability that differentiates and controls

the flow of packets based on source, destination, port, protocol, or content. They may act in concert with or contain proxy devices or similar technologies, may terminate encrypted tunnels, may do load balancing, and may perform a wide range of other audit and control functions.

- **Networks** provide for transport of data. On their own, they typically have little in the way of protection other than adequate bandwidth and redundancy to handle expected load levels and survive certain sorts of outages. Networks may have bulk-level encryption, but this only prevents physical attack on infrastructure from revealing content and provides little or no other protection.

- **Telephony** systems are used to transport data and voice and are increasingly integrated with networks in Voice-over-IP (VoIP) systems. They typically either have large connectivity and can be used to transport arbitrary data or are connected to systems to bridge otherwise secured networks and provide dynamic connectivity. Dedicated systems have very different architectures and require protection very different from other technologies in common use.

- **Backbones** are used to carry large volumes of data between main switching or routing centers. They tend to aggregate a lot of different content and form high-valued targets, but they also tend to have little or no protection other than through physical location and cable security.

- **Cabling** provides the media that carries data throughout the enterprise. It typically has physical plant, runs through cable runs of various sorts, and has to be physically secured to prevent ready and potentially high-consequence exploitation. External cabling tends to pass out of the facility boundaries and extend to remote sites through paths not physically securable by the enterprise.

- **Hosts** of various sorts are used for other purposes, such as user workstations in development environments, control systems for production facilities, personal data assistants and cellular telephones with computing capabilities, and so forth. Each has unique protection requirements and capabilities.

- **External links** connect the enterprise to the outside world and present a path for both exploitation of, and great benefit to, the enterprise.

- **Operating systems** of different sorts have different protective mechanisms designed for sets of intended uses and are commonly extended well beyond the original design purpose.

- **Configurations** are used to customize systems and platforms. Control over those configurations is critical to the protection function.

- **Applications** operate in all these environments and constitute the purpose for their existence and the basis for their utility. These applications necessarily communicate and these communications must be appropriately protected to protect the utility of the application.

- **Other technical safeguards** include a wide range of technologies that are outlined briefly under defenses.

2.4.6.9   Personnel

Personnel security issues focus on the people involved in the protection process and verify that they meet the necessary and appropriate standards and qualifications required for their duties.

- **Life cycles** associated with personnel are described in detail under life cycles .
- **Knowledge** associated with personnel helps to determine qualifications and suitability for tasks and jobs. Knowledge tends to be tracked to degrees and related programs, job history, and defined areas of expertise within the enterprise. Advanced degree programs tend to be reimbursed by the company, if job related and these are also tracked in the enterprise.
- **Awareness levels** in defined areas should be tracked to ensure that all personnel have appropriate awareness of key issues associated with their job functions and that those who are not properly qualified and aware are not permitted to do tasks that require that level of awareness. At a minimum, security awareness programs have to touch each individual in an enterprise every six months to be effective in keeping levels high enough.
- **Background checks** on all employees should be required in almost all cases. The cost can be as low as $20 for simple criminal record checks, and fairly extensive background checks can cost as little as $150. More extensive checks should be made on those with higher levels of responsibility. For some positions, such as those involving classified information or specific interactions with children, detailed background checks are required.
- **Trustworthiness** is hard to assess, but trust is often granted based on limited experience. Many of the least trustworthy people are the most trusted, because professional confidence operators are very skilled at displaying qualities that generate trust even though it is not deserved. Many companies place excessive trust in insiders and suffer the consequences. A systematic approach to evaluation of trust, including time in the position and life-related characteristics, is more effective at predicting trust-related behavior than nonmeasurable qualities associated with personal friendships and liking.
- **History** is often cited as the best predictor of future performance. Background checks and detailed information from personnel records and references tends to produce historical information about personnel that helps make reasonable and prudent decisions in this space. Missing history information on individuals in personnel records is a strong indicator of potential abuses of the system and should lead to detailed investigations.
- **Capabilities** associated with individuals help lead to their assignment to suitable tasks. Specific individuals have special talents or training that produces capabilities that are unusual or hard to train or find. These should be identified for specific information protection tasking.
- **Intents** are more difficult to understand than capabilities. However, indicated intents are often provided in letters, writings, and similar materials and should generally be explored as indicative of likely behaviors. Group

memberships and similar factors tend to indicate intent, particularly in groups with widely declared intents such as animal rights groups, ecological groups, and so forth.

- *Modus operandi* is typically associated with criminal behavior, but all people display methods of operation that tend to be reproduced over time. This is useful as an indicator for future tracking and attribution as well as for understanding how likely interactions will take place and be received.
- **Roles** are typically associated with groups of individuals and individuals may be associated with many roles, depending on their tasking within the enterprise. These roles are then translated into authorizations associated with functions on systems. People are moved from role to role as they move from job to job, with the roles fulfilled for operational continuity.
- **Changes** of employment status, job title, responsibilities, and so forth are all issues that involve information protection functions such as access to systems. Change tracking for personnel and integration into accounts in information systems, access passes, and so forth are critical to effective protection.
- **Clearances** are generally associated with individuals. These are generated through formal processes, screened by authorized screeners, and tracked and maintained by personnel systems. Clearances reflect levels of trust relative to applicable standards.
- **Need-to-know** information relates to specific work areas and projects. This too is tracked by personnel-related records and must be protected to guard projects against systematic exploitation of associated individuals.
- **IdM** (identity management) interfaces provide for interactions between the identity management system and personnel, systems, and others tasked with making decisions about individual access. They are typically integrated with personnel systems to ensure that records are up-to-date with author-itative sources.

2.4.6.10 Incident Handling

Incident handling encompasses everything from incident detection and response to disaster recovery and business continuity management. The goal of incident handling is to detect all event sequences that have potentially serious negative consequences in time to mitigate the consequences to within acceptable loss levels.

- **Detection** is central to any incident handling effort. Incidents that are not detected are not handled, and resulting consequences go unmitigated. Although some see this as relatively unimportant because undetected incidents cannot be all that harmful, history shows that these incidents may eventually become clear through extreme consequences that cannot be mitigated by that time. All detection schemes are subject to potentially unlimited numbers of false positives (false alarms) and false negatives (missed alarms). There is a trade-off between these, and the numbers of alerts can be controlled to meet the available response resources. Usually, a thresholding scheme is used to differentiate and rank alerts selected from all detections so that records may show the presence of detections that did not cause alerts but were important to understanding what happened in an investigative process. Most detection systems are not properly designed to meet the enterprise need. They are designed for technical purposes based on available data. A properly designed detection system should detect event sequences that can lead to potentially serious negative consequences and rank those event sequences as they occur by consequences and response timeliness requirements.

- **Response** systems are also very complex. For example, automated responses can be exploited for reflexive control attacks. Human intervention can be easily overwhelmed, thus producing a change in thresholds of detection and reaction and leading to serious attacks getting in "under the radar." Similar to detection, most response systems are designed for technical response and not oriented toward the needs of the enterprise. An effective system produces responses that mitigate serious negative event sequences by blocking them before the consequences exceed acceptable thresholds. Large-scale responses such as those required to mitigate harm in disasters or when business continuity plans must be invoked are disruptive and costly, so they are typically invoked only under well-defined circumstances and controlled by a well-practiced plan operated by practiced personnel.

- **Adaptation** is the long-term response to incidents that seeks to optimize enterprise performance by strategic changes not related to specific incidents but rather oriented toward changing the way classes of incidents are mitigated. A good example is the adoption of network zoning. Whereas tactical responses address stopping the current virus and cleanup operations, a strategic response to set up differentiated and separated network zones prevents large-scale worms and viruses from producing the most serious adverse consequences and inherently limits their spread and effect. These changes also reduce other risks without high costs. They are mostly architectural adaptations to environment in response to incidents.

- **OODA loops** (observe, orient, decide, and act), also known as the Boyd cycle, or similar processes exist in all detection and response systems. Observation and orientation are typically associated with the detection problem, which, in classical control theory characterizations, may be called *detection and differentiation*. Decisions and actions form the response processes. A basic idea behind the use of Boyd cycles is that the OODA loop takes time. In conflict situations, a faster OODA loop can make the difference between winning and losing. In incident handling, there are many levels of Boyd cycles, from cycles in the timeframes of seconds, associated with beating the spread rates of network worms, to cycle times in the timeframes of years, associated with adaptation processes reflected in new network architectures. Issues of timing, sensor placement and design, communications infrastructure, analytical power and technique, and actuator placement and design are all intimately tied into the Boyd cycle.

2.4.6.11 Legal Issues

Legal issues range from the inclusion of proper language in contracts to fulfillment of regulatory compliance requirements for attestation.

- **Regulatory drivers** impact all corporations. Whether your enterprise has EU privacy requirements, U.S. financial reporting requirements, U.S., Canadian, or Australian health and benefits information requirements, Chinese and French encryption requirements, or other similar requirements, regulatory drivers are increasingly forcing changes in information protection programs.
- **Civil litigation** drives many enterprises in legal areas. A good example of a protection policy that resulted in a lost civil suit comes from a recent case in which a published Web site policy guaranteed privacy of personal information. The policy was not followed and a million-dollar lawsuit was lost as a result. If there were no such policy, there would have been no such loss.
- **Criminal litigation** is pending against many executives who failed to report to shareholders on potentially serious negative consequences associated with IT failures, inadequate assurance associated with financial records, and other similar violations of law. Failures of due diligence are increasingly being treated severely because of prior executive misdeeds.
- **Notice** is required for many legal protections to be effective. A good example is trade secret and similar confidential information which has specific requirements associated with protection.
- **Contracts** with inadequate language related to information protection are widespread and result in a wide range of problems, particularly associated with access into enterprise networks used for trading partners. Customer contracts relating to records are similarly problematic. Peering agreements associated with financial and health-related information require a level of due diligence in their perfection. Safe-harbor agreements and other similar contracts require that protections be in place and effective. Many existing contracts should be updated to reflect the need to include encryption, access controls, and other protective measures in storage of exchanged information.
- **Liability** issues associated with holding information of certain types, operating systems that interact with third parties, actions of employees with respect to intellectual property, and similar information protection issues are widespread. Even an infection with a computer virus may lead to liability issues associated with the lack of due diligence in protecting peering partners from the infection. Break-ins to unpatched or unnecessarily vulnerable systems at perimeters may lead to liabilities associated with consequential damages to downstream providers and others attacked from your site.
- **Jurisdiction** is a critical issue for large multinationals; however, because of the global reach of the Internet, most businesses are international. Attacks, scams, and legal processes associated with individuals around the world are commonplace in today's information environment. A business with a Web site has presence everywhere in the world, and sales to foreign

nations may result in violations of laws that the seller or buyer are not familiar with. Jurisdictions affect legal issues across the board and mandate a dramatically more complex information protection program than would otherwise be needed.

- **Investigative** processes are linked to legal proceedings, including but not limited to legal issues associated with employee sanctions, employee rights in investigative processes, prosecutions associated with criminal acts, civil proceedings related to employee misdeeds, and all sorts of other issues.
- **Chain of custody** issues must be addressed in processes that could ultimately lead to the introduction of evidence in court. While the business-record exception in the United States generally provides for these records, other jurisdictions have varying requirements for chain of custody. Records retention processes increasingly require chain of custody to be maintained to ensure integrity of records and prevent loss of critical information that must be retained in case requested by authorities.
- **Evidential** issues come up whenever information protection issues end up in legal venues. The data presented should have adequate integrity and accuracy to ensure that it can be accepted by the courts, and it has to be presented by an expert who is responsible for those records and can attest to how they came to be and what they are supposed to represent. They have to be normal business records to be admissible under the hearsay exception, and, as a result, they must be collected in the normal course of business. Preservation orders may require that records be retained beyond their normal life cycles for evidential purposes; these orders must be followed to avoid criminal legal sanctions associated with obstruction of justice and disobeying judicial orders.
- **Forensics** efforts associated with identification, collection, preservation, analysis, and presentation of evidence in court require special training and expertise and are involved in almost all investigations associated with information protection issues.

2.4.6.12 *Physical Security*

Physical security is typically handled by the chief security officer or other individuals responsible for these issues; however, protection of information, IT, and information systems at the physical level requires special expertise and is critical to effective protection of the enterprise. Physical security is also critical for health, safety, and protection of the environment.

- **Time** has long been a central issue in physical protection and is increasingly becoming a central issue in information protection. Actions take time, whether in attack or defense, and physical security has long recognized this in the design and operation of alarm systems and response regimens. Typically, time is measured against attack graphs.
- **Location** is central to physical security issues. Different locations have different situational characteristics, such as proximity to natural hazards such as earthquakes, tsunamis, volcanoes, hurricanes, floods, lightning strikes, dust, cold, heat, and so forth. Human hazards are also associated

with location, for example, crime levels in different neighborhoods, cities, states, nations, and continents. Even the location inside office spaces leads to higher or lower profile and susceptibility to attack.

- **Paths** from the initial situation of attackers to their target and back to safety have various limitations, such as topological limits, time to penetrate barriers, equipment and skill requirements, and the number of different ways in and out of areas with and without detection and response. Paths are altered by diversions and other active attacks.
- **Properties** associated with materials, barriers, and entry and exit processes have substantial effects on available physical attack processes, time to penetrate, noise levels, detectability, and so forth.
- **Attack graphs** express the set of sequences of steps in physical attacks. They are used by attackers and defenders to determine options for entry and egress (exit) on a step-by-step basis through the successive barriers between attacker and target and target and escape (if planned). Attack graphs are also analyzed for time and equipment requirements to properly stage and time processes.
- **Entry points** include normal, emergency, forced, and surreptitious types and are typically identified with different protective measures. The entry concern is typically about who goes in, what they bring with them if they are allowed, and whether they should be where they are.
- **Egress (exit) points** are similar to entry points except that the actor is going in the other direction, and different controls are required. On exit, the concern is generally about who is leaving, if they should have been there in the first place, what is being removed, and what was left inside.
- **Emergency situations** lead to different entry and exit processes, tend to happen at higher rates with higher volume, and are prime targets for exploitation. This means that the protective process for emergency situations has to be properly adapted for those processes, or protection will be ineffective during those times. It is often easy to create an emergency and exploit the altered behaviors.
- **Hardening** of physical structures is widely used to improve protection.
- **Locking** systems of many sorts are used in physical protection. Typically, they include keyed, digital, or analog controls of electrical, mechanical, fluid, or gaseous mechanisms that are controlled based on time, location, sequence, and situation. They may have different fail-safe features and default settings, may be tamper evident, and may be redundant in different ways.
- **Mantraps** are sets of access points designed to trap individuals within them so that if they fail to properly authenticate through the entire process, they will be unable to leave until forces are able to respond. They are commonly used in physical security systems to deter repetitive entry attempts by unauthorized personnel and to catch those who break part way into a facility.
- **Surveillance** systems include coverage of a range of physical phenomena, including but not limited to audio, visual, temperature, humidity, proximity, dew point, pressure, air flow, door and window state, heat, motion, smoke, and chemical presence, absence, and level. These are connected to alarm systems, centralized or distributed data collection, analysis, and response

capabilities, may be networked, and operate together with badging and computer-related identification and authorization systems.

- **Response time** is a key issue in physical protection. Typically, response times are tuned to mitigation of consequences so that high-consequence events that demand rapid response are located close to response forces present whenever response may be needed. Response time is degraded by resource consumption and there are almost no systems designed to have adequate immediate responses to handle intentional subversion by multiple diversions.
- **Force-on-force** issues are inherent in any physical security system. Any defensive force can be overwhelmed by adequate offensive manpower and firepower.
- **OODA loops** are used to analyze physical security systems and are particularly important in understanding how small properly trained and rapid-response forces can defeat larger groups for periods of time.

As information defenses should be, physical security systems are designed to mitigate potentially serious negative consequences to acceptable levels.

2.4.6.13 Knowledge

Knowledge is particularly important as it applies to the specialized expertise required for information protection. Special information protection education, skills, mindset, and experience form critical parts of the knowledge base required to make good decisions about information protection at the design and operational levels.

- **Education** in information protection suitable to making high-quality technical decisions is highly specialized and typically associated with graduate degrees in specialty fields from accredited universities. Unfortunately, there are relatively few such graduate programs and too few graduates to fill the available positions, so highly experienced professionals with proper backgrounds may be used in their place.
- **Experience** is the best teacher in terms of not making the same mistake twice, but experience has its limits. Typical experience levels required for information protection involve one to two years per specialty area to become competent to make judgments and have broad understanding of everyday issues. With a proper educational background, the same experience is put in the context of that education, linking theory with reality, and this creates a far more effective individual, more capable of understanding the implications of events and more able to think "out of the box." Given that there are something like 25 major issues in information protection at the enterprise level, at one to two years each, the CISO should have from 25 to 50 years of relevant work experience to have the knowledge base to understand all these issues at an operational level. But technologies change over time, so although experience of 25 years ago is helpful in understanding the issues from a management perspective, it is not technically relevant at a detailed level today.

- **Training** is particularly effective for getting an individual prepared for specific tasking. The training will typically be effective at giving them the information they need for a six-month to two-year period. Once they start in the task, they will adapt to changes if they desire to and be effective for several years. If it is good training, it will also provide some of the educational background that will help them understand issues over longer timeframes. But training is not a substitute for education and should not be incorrectly associated as if it were.
- **Degrees** are often associated with expertise, but one does not need a degree to be an expert, and just having a degree does not make one an expert. There is of course a strong correlation between degrees and expertise in most fields, but not necessarily in the information protection field at this time.

2.4.6.14   Awareness

Awareness acts to ensure compliance and create identification by providing the necessary information to be able to recognize key situations and respond to them in accordance with the enterprise plan. The total set of awareness programs used throughout the enterprise provides the content used to build an effective operational security process.

- **Document review** is required for all information the employee is required to sign associated with the information protection program. Most people do not read the documents they sign in office settings, so document review is necessary to ensure that they indeed understand and agree to the terms involved.
- **Initial briefings** are required for all those who access information within an enterprise setting. These briefings lay out specifically what the user has to know in terms that they can act on. Most employees get initial employee briefings through the HR process when they first arrive to start work and this is an ideal place to include the initial information protection briefing.
- **Day-to-day** awareness is fostered by, and fosters, a properly protective work environment and culture. A goal of the CISO should be to create a culture of appropriate security through the overall program, with a central focus of cultural change and maintenance coming from the awareness program. A culture of security is not a culture of fear.
- **Department meetings** are often used to promote security and bring out protection-related issues. A fairly effective practice is for department meetings to include a review of the security failures of the last month.
- The CISO's awareness program should provide information for use in these meetings to aid in its effectiveness. This typically includes the following:
  - **A news story** from the media that relates to employees directly, such as a story about someone losing their home after an identity theft caused bad credit
  - **A current or recent situation** within the enterprise involving a security problem found and fixed or a situation that impacted a large number of employees

- Any **changes to the protection program** that has a wide-ranging effect in the enterprise
- The introduction of any **new awareness program** or other item of interest
- Any **awards or reward programs** associated with the security awareness program

- **Computer-based awareness** programs provide a limited way to test for and track awareness of specific issues in specific audiences. As a novelty it may hold interest for a time, but it rapidly becomes drudgery and should only be used as part of a systematic effort associated with specific enterprise needs that cannot be fulfilled otherwise or as a verification of awareness given via other programs.

- **Video-based awareness** programs can be viewed by large audiences or copied for large numbers of smaller audiences. If properly produced with a combination of humor, social references, and examples, it can be effective at conveying important messages in a way that causes high retention of the high-level concepts. It can be repeated periodically but becomes stale over time unless mixed in with other programs. It is expensive to produce on your own, but many such programs can be purchased for nominal fees.

- **Groups** are sometimes formed for group processes associated with security issues. These processes can be designed to build up awareness programs, but the most effective and entertaining groups of these sorts for general security awareness tend to be those formed in awareness and training game group settings.

- **Lectures** are often used by large organizations with large technical groups or other widely attended venues as a means to bring in high-quality experts to enhance internal programs. There are quite a few excellent 1-h lecturers in information protection that charge from $2500 to 10000 plus expenses per lecture.

- **Games**, typically couched as strategic scenarios and situation analyses, are often used to create policies, work through issues, and understand aspects of a space. But they have also been applied to awareness programs. Typically, a game process is used by top management to develop policies and situations, which are then played out for awareness programs by all levels of management and workers with an optional outside facilitator.

- **Posters and banners** are sometimes used to keep up awareness levels. While individual posters typically lose their effect in a few weeks, it is not expensive to put up new posters every month as part of an awareness program. Posters used in one facility can be rotated to the next facility so that a dozen different posters purchased in quantities of a few dozen each can be used to cover dozens of facilities for a year.

- **Badging and carding** systems are often associated with physical access controls, but they are also part of awareness programs. The programs should remind people that when they encounter someone without a badge, they should take action. The specific actions should be identified and employees trained. The presence and enforcement of badging and carding systems themselves are also part of keeping people aware of security as an issue.

- **Stand-downs** have been used in extreme circumstances to create awareness at a heightened level. For example, the government has used stand-downs that involve decertification of systems until they are repaired. They used the repair period to do in-depth awareness programs for all employees and contractors. In one case, tens of thousands of employees were involved in shutdowns during which awareness programs were used all day, every day, to bring the seriousness of the security issues to light.

- **Memos, e-mails, mass voice mails, internal faxes**, and similar corporate communications are often used for awareness issues, particularly when there is a critical time-sensitive issue that requires immediate notice. This may be part of the emergency notification system of the enterprise, also used in disaster recovery and other large-scale incidents. The use of these means for other aspects of awareness tends to be less effective and has the side effect of reducing the effectiveness of the emergency notification process by making it less unusual.

- **Award programs** provide ways to make information protection activities positive experiences and generate social benefits to those who do these aspects of their job well. Awards programs can be run for a few thousand dollars per year and typically include plaques or paper certificates, public notice, notice at department meetings, and free dinners for two at local restaurants or other similar items.

- **Social pressure** is applied by creating a culture that encourages secure behaviors. For example, when someone unrecognized is in a workspace, the employees who normally occupy that space should know that their responsibility is to go over and say hello, introduce themselves, and find out if they can help the newcomer. If newcomers are not forthcoming with useful information about who they are, if they do not have a proper badge, or if they are otherwise suspicious, the social environment should create the response that ultimately leads to their being escorted out of the facility, arrested, or otherwise handled. If this is the social environment, security will be effective and people will be friendly, but if it is not, penetration of the facility for long-term access will be easily achieved and sustained. Creating a social awareness program is a good foundation for the material included in the other aspects of the awareness program and leads to both compliance and identification.

- **Covert awareness programs** have recently been noticed by advertisers and adopted for selling. They involve surreptitiously planting individuals within environments to create social changes. This may take the form of someone who displays protective behaviors in conjunction with a planted intruder, someone who creates a "buzz" around a new idea or program, or someone who uses any of a wide range of other influence tactics to move group behavior toward desired objectives.

2.4.6.15 Organization

Organizational issues are handled by the power and influence associated with the overall protection program and its leadership:

- **Structure** is used and changed to provide direct or indirect control over behaviors and motivations. It may involve moving managers out of their positions when they fail to cooperate with the program, going to a matrix management system to allow the CISO's organization to more directly control select employees, the creation of new governance bodies to create social pressures at the management level, and so forth.
- **Rewards** at an organizational level are typically out of kilter with protection objectives in enterprises without effective programs. An effective program alters the enterprise reward structure so that employees who show excellence in protection functions are rewarded with raises and promotions. Working on an information security issue should be seen as a path to advancement and might be considered a requirement for promotion into certain positions. Performance reviews should include explicit performance relative to information protection and proper behavior should be rewarded in clear ways.
- **Punishments** associated with poor security performance should include negative management reviews, sanctions of various sorts, and, ultimately, termination and prosecution depending on the specifics. Security should be included as a normal part of employee reviews, and these should be based on performance metrics fed into the overall information protection program's measurement process.
- **Communication** is at the heart of organizational interaction and is a key success factor for the CISO. Creating and maintaining lines of communication throughout the enterprise and using those lines to effect control and observe behaviors is fundamental to success.

2.4.6.16   Summary of Perspectives

Taken in conjunction, these organizational issues form the basis for control of the enterprise information protection system. They interact across the enterprise and form the heart of the enterprise information protection system.

2.5 Control Architecture

The control architecture creates the overarching objectives and structural approaches to protection without drilling down into the details of how those objectives are met or approaches are implemented. It is a theoretical structure that ultimately gets implemented by the technical security architecture.

2.5.1 Protection Objectives

Although the overall objective of information protection is to manage risk in the business, at a more detailed level, specific objectives have been identified that help to achieve this overall objective. They are typically codified as integrity, availability, confidentiality, use control, and accountability. These objectives exist in the context of interdependencies, and they are associated with technologies used to assist in achieving them.

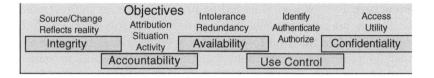

2.5.1.1   Integrity

In most cases, the integrity of information is most important to its utility because, even if it is available and kept confidential, properly audited, and under use control, if it is wrong, its utility is poor. If it is wrong in specific ways, it can be very harmful. Integrity is often broken down into the integrity of the source of information, protection from inappropriate or unauthorized changes in the content, and assurance that the content represents an accurate reflection of reality suitable for the purpose. Source integrity expresses the association of reliability of content with its source and is an example of the correspondence of the content with reality. Many cryptographic technologies are associated with integrity in the sense of freedom from unauthorized change and attribution to source; however, cryptography has serious limitations in integrity protection. Change control is a vital component of an effective integrity control scheme because it provides redundancy-based controls over changes to verify that they are reasonable, appropriate to the need, and that they operate correctly in the environment before the changes are deployed. Changes also have potentially recursive, complex, and indirect effects that lead to unintended consequences. For example, computer viruses use changes in software to cause transitive spread of the virus from program to program. This is an unintended but predictable consequence of combining general-purpose function with transitive information flow and sharing. Integrity technologies indicated in the diagram include the following:

- **Redundancy** allows faults to be detected and, sometimes, corrected.
- **Validation** provides the means to increase assurance through independent (redundant) confirmations or refutations of form.
- **Consistency** checks use redundancy to validate data.
- **Verification** provides the means to increase assurance through independent (redundant) confirmations or refutations of content.
- **Multisource** verification provides specific a sort of independent confirmation or refutation.
- **Multifactor** approaches use independent sorts of measurements or factors to independently verify content.
- **Trust models** are sometimes created and applied to provide metrics on trust.
- **Submit/commit cycles** provide independent confirmation over an independent channel.
- **Watermarking** is used to provide a self-validation of the media on which content is sent.

- **Cryptographic checksums** provide redundancy that allows validation of use of specific keys or confirmation of content against published coded values. These are typically many-to-one functions that are harder to forge than the material they cover.
- **Integrity shells** are real-time just before use verifications of content, typically, against cryptographic checksums.
- **Digital signatures** allow validation of use of private keys.
- **Certificates** provide validation of the authority to sign based on an authoritative third-party source.
- **Trusted Computer System Evaluation Criteria (TCSEC)** systems use high-surety access controls to ensure flow control and limit corruption.
- **Trusted Computing Group (TCG)** systems use integrity shells, cryptographic checksums, and similar methods to ensure the integrity of process lineage.

2.5.1.2 Availability

If information is not available in a timely fashion, its utility decreases but may not completely disappear. Availability is typically measured in terms of mathematical formulas for availability and reliability of the function when needed. Availability is typically measured as percentage of downtime per unit time. For example, hours of system outage per year is used for some systems. Sometimes, it is normalized for utility in the enterprise, such as the use of user outage hours per month. It can also be calculated based on mean time to failure (MTTF) and mean time to repair (MTTR) as MTTR/(MTTF + MTTR). Assuming that everything is properly accounted for, these are measurements after the fact, but not as useful for prediction, which is critical for design.

- **Interdependency analysis** is used to determine availability of systems based on availability of other systems they depend on. It is central to the analysis of availability, even though it is often ignored.
- **Redundancy** is used to increase availability by making independent resources available in case of failure. Generally, redundancy increases availability but reduces reliability. That is, there will be more failures, but the percentage of time with uncovered failures will be lower. Redundancy must be carefully implemented to avoid brittleness and common-mode failures.
- **Higher-quality components** are also effective at increasing availability. The approach of using higher quality implies a trade-off between the cost of quality and the cost of quantity associated with redundancy.

2.5.1.3 Confidentiality

If confidentiality is lost, some sorts of information may become useless or even dangerous, but this is rarely the case. In most cases, there is some potential liability and not much more. Confidentiality is usually controlled based on clearance of the identity, the certainty of the authentication of that identity, the classification of the content, and the need for the authorized purpose. The means of creating and operating this basis is often more easily attacked than the real-time protective system at the operating system or application level.

- **Information flow controls** are the only really effective way to limit the movement of information from place to place. All other techniques are leaky in one way or another, and most can be defeated to great effect by any reasonably astute attacker. These controls are implemented at routers through network separation technologies (e.g., VLANs with quality of service controls to eliminate covert channels), in computer systems through access controls, in physical technologies by separation of systems and networks by distance and with shielding, and in applications through application-level access control.

- **TCSEC systems** are systems implemented under the trusted computer system evaluation control and are designed and rated relative to their ability to correctly implement flow controls. High TCSEC ratings imply a high degree of certainty that flows from more sensitive to less sensitive areas only pass through covert channels. If used in limited applications, as in network control devices, they can be highly effective at allowing only specific sorts of controlled flows. However, covert channels are found in all such systems, and for general-purpose use, they are subject to virus attack, with the viruses then carrying covert channel exploitation code. TCSEC systems are often given as examples of how confidentiality control depends on integrity control for its effectiveness.

- **Cryptography** is often used as a separation mechanism to prevent those who gain access to data from meaningfully using the content it represents. Cryptographic systems are hard to get right, typically have many covert channels, key distribution issues, recovery issues, performance issues, and are hard to manage on a large scale; however, there are significant products in the market that greatly ease this burden at a substantial financial cost.

- **Abyss processors** and similar containment devices are special-purpose physically hardened devices used for high-surety processing. They use physical security barriers in typically small devices such as smart cards and other similar platforms to provide special-purpose functions, for example, cryptographic key management and commit components of submit/commit cycles. They are costly to develop but effective in providing secrecy for small amounts of data leveraged to secure larger volumes of data. FIPS certification demonstrates high quality in these systems, critical for high-consequence uses.

- **TCG systems** use standardized specifications to implement abyss processors within normal computing platforms. They are predominantly used for authentication and encryption and address many of the recovery issues at relatively low cost (about a few dollars) per computer.

- **Digital diodes** are separation mechanisms that allow one-directional information flow. They are designed so that less secret or higher-integrity information can be passed to more secret or lower-integrity areas without the potential for the more secret or lower-integrity information passing back to or affecting the less secure or higher-integrity area. Thus, they provide the basic mechanisms for one-directional information flow. They have no covert channels in high-surety implementations and known and identifiable covert channels in lower-surety implementations.

2.5.1.4 Use Control

If use control is lost, either information is not usable by those who are supposed to be able to use it, which corresponds to a loss of availability, or information is usable by those would should not be able to use it. This can lead to loss of integrity, availability, or confidentiality, depending on the specifics of the uses permitted. Use control generally associates authentication requirements associated with identified parties for authorized uses. The basic notion underlying use control is that identified individuals or systems acting on their behalf are granted appropriate use based on their identity and the extent to which they have demonstrated that identity to be authentic. If the current level of authentication is inadequate to the need, additional authentication is required to meet the level required for the use.

- **Biometrics** are used to provide authentication based on physical characteristics typically associated with individuals out of a group.
- **Something you have** like a smart card, securID card, universal serial bus (USB) authentication device, proximity card, radio frequency identification (RFID) tag, or other devices are used for authentication.
- **Passwords**, pass phrases, and other similar mechanisms based on user knowledge, skills, and capabilities are used to indicate something the user knows or can do.
- **Separation of duties** is fundamental to the administration of use and acts as a control over potential abuses. Separation of duties is typically operated without consideration for time; however, time transitivity of use is critical to proper separation. As a simple example, the requirement to separate purchasing from payments is based on preventing a single individual from placing an order and paying for that order. This can be exploited to pay the person or a relative based only on the individual's own stipulation. Without time transitivity controls, a person who works in purchasing today can get a job in accounts payable at a later date, perhaps at a different facility and under a different name, and carry out the rest of the fraud. To counter such attacks, which have been perpetrated in the past, life-cycle tracking of individuals and uses associated with those individuals is necessary.
- **Process controls** limit how processes can proceed. An excellent example of a failed approach to process control is the placement of purchasing and payables in the same computer system. Even if separation of duties is applied to the people who work in AP and Purchasing, the systems administrator of the system can typically violate the process controls to gain access to both capabilities. The administrator might directly place purchase orders and payments into the database, thus avoiding the

programmed controls that exist to prevent normal users from doing so through normal program interfaces. This is why change control is required for such systems and why separation and process controls must go beyond the boundaries of any individual person or computer system.

- **Submit/commit systems** are use control devices that separate the preparation of a transaction from its approval process. If properly implemented, a device is used for taking the submitted information and committing the transaction, and that device is physically separated, unforgeable, uncircumventable, and independently controlled.

- **Roles and rules** are often used to associate individuals with the roles they play to perform their job functions. Rules are applied both to the allocation of people to roles and the actions permitted by people in those roles. This abstraction layer permits organizations to create processes independent of individuals, allows easy changes of people associated with roles, and reduces administrative effort associated with maintaining individual access by replacing it with a two-step process of (1) maintaining roles and rules and (2) associating people with roles. This abstraction reduces management complexity, but care must be taken to ensure that it does not prevent proper accountability and that time transitivity of role assignment is done at finer granularity. Roles and rules also tend to aggregate risks unless properly controlled.

- **Identity management** (IdM) infrastructure provides a means by which role, rules, identification, authentication, and authorization processes can be joined together in an administrative mechanism and functional infrastructure elements. By doing this, IdM also tends to aggregate risks so that the IdM infrastructure rapidly rises to a higherrisk category as it gains efficiency by centralizing use control and audit functions.

2.5.1.5   Accountability

Loss of accountability reduces the certainty with which proper operation can be verified either now or in the future. Accountability is often considered in terms of attribution of actions to actors, the accurate identification and recording of the situation, and the association of the activity with the actor in the situation.

- **Attribution** of actions to actors is particularly problematic; however, we generally use user identity information associated with authentication processes to assert attribution (to a level of certainty associated with the authentication process) of actions associated with the identity (to a level of certainty associated with the surety of the systems and infrastructures involved) to the individual associated with the identity (to a level of surety associated with the initial registration process, background checks, and surety of the systems that maintain and promulgate the identity information). Of course, this begs the issue of how certain we are of each of these elements and leads to a level of uncertainty associated with any accountability process, particularly such a process that might be subject to internal malicious attack.

- **Audit trails** are the reflections of the attribution of actions to actors in tangible form. These records are generated by various systems and functional elements of applications and sent to storage and recording media for retention, transfer, evaluation, and other use. The storage and recording media are subject to attack and may reside in the same system as the audits are generated, or elsewhere. It may be append and read-only, may pass through protective barriers, and may be well controlled — or it may not. Surety of the audit process limits surety of accountability. Audit trails tend to record specific information thought to be of value to the need, but they may not be useful for situations in which systems are not used as designed. For example, in a direct attack against the operating system leading to a modification of the underlying database files, the accountability mechanisms of the database engine are often circumvented, leaving no audit of changes.
- **Granularity** issues drive to limits on accountability. A seemingly simple transaction, such as the movement of money from account to account might seem simple and readily accounted for. But if this transaction involves remote Internet access to a Web server that uses a back-end application server to modify data in a mainframe database that stores results in a storage area network, the number of auditable events could easily run into the tens or even hundreds. Every system involved and every aspect of their operation may result in an audit record.
- **Analysis** issues associated with audit trails include timing, correlation of the many audit trails associated with any transaction, identification and explanation of excess or missing audit trails, accounting for failure modes and the results of all such modes when they occur, reconstruction of events from partial audit records, and protection of confidentiality associated with the data the audit trails reflect. The analysis process must not be capable of corrupting or deleting the audit records or many other problems occur. Audit trails may be correlated for data aggregation and this, too, must be understood in context to determine what separation of duties and use controls over audit information is required.
- **Preservation** issues are driven by a combination of organizational and legal requirements. Legal requirements call for retention of accountability information of many sorts, particularly those associated with business records. Retention periods vary but 7 years is the minimum period. The ability to identify and retain specific records associated with incidents or legal matters for longer periods is also required. Some accounting records must be destroyed in a timely fashion in order to follow EU regulations and other privacy requirements, so a method for separating different audit records based on retention and protection requirements becomes a critical part of the accountability process.

2.5.2 Access Control Architecture

Access control is used to implement the basis controls that assure integrity, availability, confidentiality, use control, and accountability. Based on individuals with clearances and classifications of content and systems in terms of consequence, use is limited. Use control dictates that use should only be granted to content and systems based on need, thus the principle of least privilege applies and use-based compartments extend between different consequence levels. In addition, compart-

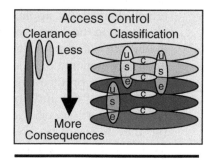

ments may be made based on the desire to limit risk aggregation. Controls (c) are placed between levels of consequence to assure to a desired degree of certainty that consequence levels do not interact except in well defined and properly controlled ways. These controls are implemented through combinations of physical and informational functional units.

2.5.3 Technical Architecture Functional Units and Composites

The technical architecture is made up of composites formed from functional units that are themselves composites. Functional units are made up of layered sets of protective barriers and functional applications that take input and initial state and produce output and next state. These units are controlled through a control plane and audited to an audit plane; they may send queries and get replies associated with external data sources. Surety increases as more layers are passed, because each layer can independently have a failure and yet layers are independent of each other in the sense that they do not directly connect to each other. They do pass state and error information back and forth, and the audit process can detect behaviors that exceed normal functional unit behavior. Typical layers include firewalls to eliminate clearly invalid inputs and sources, decryption and authentication, data input validation, state machine modeling for proper context, identity-based access controls, validation of queries and replies against known valid classes, redundant sourcing of data based on requirements, back-end process selection for the query and reply process, encryption and authentication for back end processing, and verification of results from queries.

2.5.4 Perimeter Architectures

Perimeters are implemented in both physical and logical senses, with logical perimeters often placed at physical perimeters for the added surety associated with their co-location. For example, a

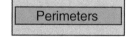

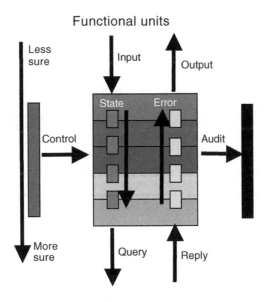

cryptographic mechanism might be placed at the physical barrier between an enclave and the outside world so that from inside the enclave only plaintext is visible and from outside the enclave only ciphertext is visible. By locating the mechanism at the physical barrier, there is no chance that a cross connection between the two sides will occur because the physical protection prohibits it. Similarly, the encryption makes the physical barrier more effective at separation because there is a reduction in the logical mechanisms that can be applied to bypass the encryption mechanism.

Perimeters are often judged by the set of barriers present against illegitimate passage, the quality of implementation of those barriers, and the ease of passage for legitimate purposes.

2.5.4.1   Physical Perimeter Architecture

Physical controls are integrated into informational controls. For deterrence there are signs, terrain, location, and deceptions. For prevention, perimeters use a wide range of barricades including, but not limited to, steps, fences, cement separators, moats, mounds, walls, and even mine fields. Detection involves a wide range of sensor technologies including visual, infrared, ultrasonic, sonic, chemical, pressure, motion, and even animal mechanisms. Reaction involves the movement of forces or use of fires of various sorts. Adaptation is undertaken by structural redesigns, movement of facilities, increased or enhanced perimeters, and so forth.

World Location / Mapping / Accessibility / Deceptions / Response forces & times	
Property Perimeters / Signs / Entry paths / Barriers / Sensors / Response forces	
Perimeter Construction / Signs / Deceptions / Entry paths / Barriers / Sensors Emergency modes / Response forces and times	
Facility Construction / Zones / Flow paths / Barriers / Sensors Emergency modes / Response forces and times	

2.5.4.1.1 World

Different technologies are typically placed at different places. For example, concealment of location by not advertising it or putting signs on doors or putting an address in the corporate directory are effective at limiting the number of people who know where a facility is, but this really only works for those who do not have legitimate access. Some locations are in remote areas making them inaccessible for most people who don't have a good reason to be there, and this forms an extensive distance barrier to approach without detection. Modern mapping capabilities provide global positioning system–based maps and overhead satellite photography so that preventing the mapping of an area is far harder than it was many years ago when simply not putting streets within a land area on the map would prevent it from being mapped by hostiles. Deceptions of all sorts, ranging from false locations in directories to addresses that don't seem to be there to concealment of a facility within another business, have all been successful at limiting the knowledge of attackers of a target. Response forces and times associated with their responses are also key to the analysis of location. For example, being located near emergency services provides increased security through decreased response times.

2.5.4.1.2 Property

Property location and characteristics such as grades, soil makeup, weather, and surrounding topology are important factors in the protective function played by the property on which a facility is placed. Properties in flood zones, at the end of airport runways, on known fault lines, next to active volcanoes, in tsunami areas, below large bodies of water, near hazardous chemical plants or explosives factories, and in other paths of natural or unnatural disasters are subject to the extreme probabilities associated with those locations and require additional protective measures in order to achieve the same level of protection that would commonly be afforded by a different location. Perimeters surrounding properties and property lines with natural barriers, barriers within properties such as rivers, lakes, arroyos, cliffs, and similar natural and unnatural barriers are important to characterizing attack graphs into and out of properties. Accessibility from the air, ground, water, and underground are all important to understanding attack paths as well.

2.5.4.1.3 Perimeter

Perimeters surrounding properties and within properties provide distance and distance has advantages. Distance implies time in physical movement, also reducing electromagnetic, sonic, and other emanation levels. It increases power levels required for exfiltration of data, makes running wires take longer and cost more, makes it more obvious when someone tries to go from one side of the perimeter to the other, and makes it harder to tunnel under or fly above without being detected.

Barriers of various sorts are typified by moats and walls. They provide added reduction in emanations of various sorts, perhaps blocking visual inspection from easy-to-enter proximate locations. They prevent penetration by different sorts of mechanisms ranging from a simple fence that prevents walk-ins to a barrier capable of deflecting a high explosive blast. They also provide cover for attackers who may be able to hide behind or between barriers to defeat detection.

For the vast majority of cases, barriers have to be permeable to be useful because some amount of legitimate use has to pass into and out of the protected area. Entry paths are provided to allow barriers to be bypassed in controlled ways and under proper identification and authentication processes that grant authorization to pass. Mantraps and similar technologies may be employed to trap individuals who try to pass a barrier without authorization to do so, but there are liability issues and potential criminal liabilities associated with this sort of restraint in some situations. For volume entry and exit facilities, entry paths have to be fairly direct, proximate to parking or entrances, and able to handle the volumes required. Construction of barriers and emergency modes for bypassing barriers are critical to understanding behaviors under unusual circumstances as opposed to normal operational modes.

Signs are commonly required to provide legal notice as to trespass, proper entry, authorized access and use, and safety and health hazards associated with the property. Sensors around and within properties can be very helpful in allowing smaller numbers of people to more rapidly detect and triage attempted entries and passage. A wide range of sensor technologies are available, ranging from unified heat, sound, light, motion, shape, humidity, temperature, and dew point sensor arrays to simple trip wires and touch-sensitive devices that sound alarms. Response forces are required in order for these methods to be effective with the time required for response at different force levels acting as a critical factor in the effectiveness against specific threats.

2.5.4.1.4 Facility

Facilities have topologies that dictate how things and people go from place to place, internal barriers, sensors, zones, and similar protective mechanisms that are analogous to those on properties, but typically with better controls. For example, buildings often have sound, temperature, and humidity controls, motor generators, doors of different quality with locks of different quality and hinges on one side or the other. Construction materials and processes dictate the classes of threat capable of bypassing barriers such as walls and doors as a function of time, with and without detection. Passage under floors, over ceilings, through air ducts, by picking or tricking locks, electrically or mechanically fooling sensors or tripping opening mechanisms, removing or cutting hinges from doors — all grant human access. Tailgating, introduction of noxious gases to invoke emergency modes, fires, floods, and any number of other reflexive control attacks may be induced or occur by accident. Response forces and times also limit the time for an attack.

2.5.4.2 *Logical Perimeter Architecture*

Logical perimeters act in much the same way as physical perimeters, providing a series of barriers that slow or stop attackers. They include transforms and separation mechanisms at the outer perimeters, access controls, transforms, enclaves, and filters at facilities perimeters, and a range of other technologies closer into the higher valued content.

2.5.4.2.1 World

From the outside world, perimeter mechanisms are generally oriented toward things that permit the perimeters to be permeated with relative safety. Virtual private networks (VPNs) are used to provide encrypted tunnels between areas while authentication technologies are designed to allow the identity to be authenticated to the degree appropriate for the use. Submit-commit mechanisms provide physically secured devices to the user (to the desired level of surety) so that any mechanism desired can be used to submit a request but an adequately secured method is used to commit to that use. Enterprise rights management is used to pack protective mechanisms with content for low surety levels and can be used at a distance. Trusted computing bases (TCBs) can be used to provide higher assurance at remote locations.

2.5.4.2.2 Facility

Facility-level protection typically includes mandatory access controls at the network level, low-level communications card or processor identification and authentication mechanisms for devices attaching to internal networks and systems, VPN termination or internal VPN capabilities, physically secured logical network separation perimeters such as virtual local area networks

| **World** |
| VPN / Submit-commit / Encrypt / ERM / Authenticate / TCB |

| **Facilities** |
| MAC / NAC / VPN / Perimeter / FW / NIDRS / GW / Proxy / Audit |

| **Data Center** |
| MAC / NAC / VPN / FW / Perimeters / NIDRS / GW / Proxy / Audit |
| Query limits / Separation of duties / Redundancy / IdM / CC / Testing |

| **Zones** |
| FW / Perimeter / Audit / Control / NIDRS / Filters / Transforms / |
| Risk aggregation controls / Separation of duties / CC / testing |

(VLANs), firewalls, network intrusion and anomaly detection and response systems, gateway systems, proxy servers, and audit mechanisms.

2.5.4.2.3 Data Center

Data centers typically have additional protections both at the physical level in terms of internal areas within facilities, and at the network and logical level in terms of similar protections to those for the facility but with tighter settings and more restrictions. Additional protective measures include query limits that limit the syntax and semantics of database queries, separation of duties protections to assure that risk aggregation is limited from a logical perspective within the data centers, redundancy for increased assurance levels against denial of services or single points of failure, identity management systems and interfaces to increase the surety of and specificity of access control decisions, change control mechanisms to increase the surety of software and configurations for systems with higher valued content for utilities or aggregations of lower valued content that form medium or high risks, and more extensive testing processes.

2.5.4.2.4 Zones

Zones are used to further separate portions of networks at a logical level both from a standpoint of classification and need to know as implied by the access control architecture, and from a standpoint of disaggregation of risks, separation of control from data, and other protective requirements associated with functional unit design and risk management requirements. Zones are implemented with firewalls and other perimeter mechanisms, audit mechanisms, control mechanisms, and separation of audit from control from content. Network anomaly and intrusion detection and response systems may be used along with filtering technologies such as virus detection and transform technologies such as those identified for content control to augment solutions in some areas. Separation of duties tends to be implemented so that different individuals have responsibilities in different zones, and this helps with risk aggregation controls as well. Change control and testing processes are also varied depending on the specific needs of the zones as defined.

2.5.4.3   Perimeter Summary

While perimeter technologies vary widely they have some commonalities that define their utility at an architectural level. While a boundary may have substantial size, perimeter mechanisms tend to operate at a boundary and not within that boundary. As a result, perimeter architecture is oriented toward the fundamental notion of what will pass the barrier in what direction at what rate and how long the barrier will withstand what sorts of forces. Put in other terms, the barriers act to either sever attack graphs or increase the time to traverse links of the attack graph depending on the capabilities being used in order to defeat it. At the same time, it is desirable that perimeters provide as little friction to normal operation as possible, and for high volume perimeters such as airport entrances or network perimeters, their design must facilitate low delay times under high load.

2.5.5 Access Process Architecture

The utility of the overall information capability of the enterprise depends on the ability to legitimately access the information resources with minimal friction while still assuring the continuing value of the information in light of the hostilities of the environment in which it works. The access process architecture defines how identified

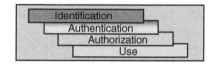

subjects demonstrate their identities through authentication, and how the properly authenticated identified subjects can then use the content through an authorization mechanism.

2.5.5.1   Identification

Identity of people and things, including programs and processes, is in itself a purely informational item. It is a, hopefully unique, tag that allows an individual to be associated with other properties. An identification system is a system used to track identities and associate them with these other properties. Initialization of identification processes is fundamental to their success as this is the process by which those things are associated with their identifying set of properties. For low surety situations, anybody will do, but clearance processes with background checks and detailed life reviews are invoked for situations in which people have to be identified with higher surety upon entry to a system of identification while pedigree for hardware and software is commonly considered in determining its suitability for trust in high risk situations. Once an identity and some of its properties have been established the identification system can provide a wide range of additional utility.

2.5.5.2   Authentication

Authentication is a process by which an identity can be verified as authentic by a process of testing that identity against the properties known for it in the identification system. For example, the identification system may have a user name and password associated with a human individual, in which case the presentation of those authentication factors are usable for authentication of the identity. The surety of the authenticity of an identification depends on the available properties in the identification system and the ability to present and verify those factors as present or absent in the individual in question. For higher risk, higher surety is typically desired, and sequential authentications may be used to increase the certainty with which authenticity of an identity is believed. Different properties have different surety levels and withstand different threats more or less successfully. For example, biometrics are measures of what something is based on physical properties such as fingerprints, hand shape, eye print, DNA patterns, footfall pattern, and so forth. Fingerprints don't normally change and are unique to the individual, which makes them good for authentication; however, they can also be easily forged by skilled attackers.

2.5.5.3   Authorization

Once a subject's identity has been authenticated to an adequate level for a decision process to be completed, that subject may be authorized to a certain use. The authorization process typically involves matching a requested use with the identity and surety of authentication to determine how that attempt at use should be treated. Many treatments are possible depending on circumstances and capabilities of the protective system in use. Some options include: permit the use, refuse the use with a reason given, require additional authentication for that use, require additional authorization for that use through an approval process, refuse that use and act to eliminate further requests, redirect the request to a deception system, and audit the request and its resolution. The decision on what to do is typically driven by some sort of table that associates authorities with subjects. This may involve a system or roles and rules used to determine what functions are allowed to what roles with the roles associated with the individual identities as a second step in the process. Such a system facilitates changes more efficiently by allowing roles to be changed for identities at a high rate and roles to change at a lower rate, allows checking of roles against separation of duties requirements and similar overarching needs, and provides a reduction in errors and delays associated with changing permissions for large groups or individuals.

2.5.5.4   Use

Use is the business utility that this process is designed to facilitate. As a result, the process should be relatively transparent and automatic to the user relative to the utility associated with that use. So the amount of effort and surety required for doing something simple like checking the time of day should, in most circumstances, be minimal. Otherwise, the effort required to perform the process exceeds the business value granted. In most cases, authentication allows use of a set of capabilities for a period of time so that a single authenticated identity is authorized for sets of activities, which are performed without additional authentication at every step. For high-valued transactions, such as large financial transfers or setting off explosive devices, additional authentication is warranted and applied; however, the additional authentication associated with that high-valued transaction may also be leveraged to allow uninhibited subsequent use for a period of time and to a set of functions. Use over time from locations, and within other contexts may be highly limited, but in most cases large ranges of usage in excess of least privilege requirements are granted because of the complexity of limiting use at a fine granularity. In these cases the audit mechanisms associated with use are often used to provide additional checks on that use and to limit the effects of illicit use. In all cases, use should be audited if the value of the operation exceeds the threshold of risk requiring audit or if there are regulatory or other drivers that mandate auditing of use.

2.5.6 Change Control Architecture

Change control processes designed to assure that, with increasing surety for increasing consequences, changes to production systems are throughly tested, verified to meet the need and contain no inappropriate code, work properly on test data, and can be reverted to previous states 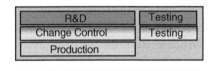 and operate properly under emergency conditions. These verification and testing processes involve administrative and technical actions, usually involve a tracking process and ticketing system, require special expertise and technology, and are supposed to precisely reflect the production environment. In some disaster recovery programs, the testing environment is kept at a separate site and used as the emergency recovery environment.

2.5.6.1   Research and Development

Research and development includes all programming activities and is typically carried out by programmers who have specific design and implementation goals. For change controlled environments, the changes made by programmers are limited to changes associated with the desired change in functionality of behavior of the mechanisms being changed. Programmers are normally responsible for testing their changes against functional requirements and security requirements as well as against historical fault types. These are called *regression tests*.

2.5.6.2   Change Control

Once research and development completes its changes, the change control process evaluates those changes to assure that they are (1) necessary to meet the defined change in functional requirements, (2) appropriate to the changes functional requirements, (3) of no material affect on any other functional properties not identified as part of the change, (4) obvious and well understood in their operation, (5) consisting of only source code and meaningful data, and (6) consistent with proper operation of the changed system. The changes that pass these tests are then tested against operational requirements, security requirements, and with regression tests. If they fail these tests, they are returned to research and development and the failures identified with the individuals responsible. Failures of this sort should be used as a negative performance indicator on personnel reviews, and managers who fail to react to such failures seriously should also be subject to negative performance reviews. Repeated failures of this sort should result in termination. Reversion copies should be kept and reversion tested.

2.5.6.3   Production

In production use, programs do not change and their status should be regularly verified. Unauthorized changes should be investigated and causes eliminated. Failures in production should lead to reversion if they are high consequence.

2.6   Technical Security Architecture

2.6.1   Issues of Context

Context is important to almost all decisions in information protection. Context generally includes the basic questions of who, what, where, how, when, and why as they relate to information, systems, infrastructures, people, and functions.

2.6.1.1   Time ("When")

Time is important in tracking behavior, associating events across infrastructure, and making determinations about what is authorized and over what period something happened. It is also a central issue in all processes, particularly in attack and defense processes where time is of the essence and OODA-loop timing issues may determine outcomes.

- **Zone**: The time zone associated with the action under consideration. This is the common time people think of and deal with on a day-to-day basis.
- **Time**: The time within a context, or more commonly, the universal coordinated time (UTC) associated with the item of interest. UTC is the time typically used internally in system clocks and many applications and audit systems. It is useful for getting a common context to compare systems in diverse locations. In outer space and under-sea systems, time may be kept in some frame of reference, and UTC is commonly used.
- **Context**: In some situations, time is relative to context, and this must be expressed in those situations where there might be a difference. For example, mission-oriented systems tend to keep time in the relative context of the mission.
- **Accuracy**: Time bases have different errors type and magnitudes. For example, average error, skew, and skew rate are frequent issues in times based on line frequency commonly used in electric clocks.
- **Differential**: Differential time is a common issue in synchronization and differential limits are critical to many times operations.

2.6.1.2   Location ("Where")

Location historically dominated access control, but mobility has made location harder to determine, the mobile and remote work force has caused location to become harder to limit, and location-independent approaches to computing are increasingly deployed. The utility of location has changed but not disappeared.

- **Network location** determines large-scale controls to a large extent. Zoning policies are generally effective over locations with different locations in the topology granted different sorts of access. Whereas some networks in the general sense allow broad locational deviation, others are still located within physical enclosures or in limited areas.
- **Address**, whether related to a map location or an Internet protocol or other similar sort of address, is a common method for differentiating systems and uses. Within banks, for example, teller functions can only be undertaken from select access points, and this can still often be determined based on addresses.
- **Lines** associated with telephone systems, terminal connectors, and direct or switched communications systems are very widely used to indicate location and this location is then used to determine controls.
- **Numbers**, often special phone numbers, are used for maintenance access. They are often restricted to select remote telephone numbers.
- **Global Positioning System** (GPS) locations are used in increasing numbers of systems to provide location information that can be correlated with other factors to provide information ranging from routing to assistance

calls. GPS has been used to limit access and to provide location-based authentication. Location can also be correlated with time for travel rates and to associate physical and logical access.

- **Physical locations** are associated with devices and protective barriers and are often used as a basis for allowing or denying access. Known physical locations may have known protective conditions that allow extraordinary access based on facilities protection, personnel characteristics, and so forth. Local access to consoles is commonly used to grant maintenance access.
- **Logical location** codifies conditions associated with a device or operating environment used to associate a level of trust. Typically, proxy servers or similar mechanisms provide a local presence that is used to gain access from another location.
- **Delta** expresses the accounting for location changes that is sometimes used to determine physical possibility and other related conditions. For example, a credit card presented on the West Coast of the United States and then presented again on the East Coast of Africa an hour later cannot be the same card under current transportation systems. Misrepresentation is happening.

2.6.1.3 Purpose ("Why")

Controls based on reasons are fairly rare in the sense that the controls are rarely tied directly to purpose, however, this is implemented indirectly in many systems by associating a purported purpose to specific usage patterns. As a rule of thumb, and as a prudent practice, unless there is an affirmative reason to grant access, access should be denied.

- **Authority** is usually allowed as a basis for authorization. The purpose is to fulfill the mandates of positional power.
- **Context** leads to use. For example, access to a database with financial records is granted to processes within applications acting for users who normally would not have access in order to provide them with prices for goods being sold.
- **Applicability** of an action to a purpose is the basis for allowing use, while risk associated with access is a reason for denying use. As there is always a level of risk involved in any action, a level of applicability required for access must be defined in order to grant access.
- **Basis** expresses the underlying rationale that justifies use. It is typically expressed in terms of a rationale that makes sense to the owner of the thing being used. Typically, the basis dictates the decision process over use. However, as this is not readily codifiable in computer terms, human judgments over classes of uses and applications authorized for those uses is substituted, at the cost of accuracy but to the advantage of easier decision-making.
- **Rationale** typically consists of a logical argument of some sort that balances risks against benefits.

- **Explanation** is used to provide additional details to the decision-maker. This is used after the fact to validate the decisions when independent reviews are undertaken and in periodic and situation-specific reviews.
- **Validity** of explanations, rationale, and basis are subject to external inspection. For example, if the basis is a rationale using an explanation that doesn't make logical sense, or the rationale depends on a fact that is not accurate, the basis is not valid and use should not be granted.

2.6.1.4   Behaviors ("What")

Behaviors are particularly useful and increasingly important in the making of protection-related decisions, either the behaviors of individuals or the behaviors of systems. Whereas the science of understanding behaviors is old, it is not precise, and there is much left to do in this area.

- **Actions** are tracked in behavioral modeling and analysis systems and the actions taken are used to make protection decisions.
- **Sequences** of actions are particularly informative because, in many cases, attacks are composed of sequences of actions that individually seem benign.
- **Situations** dictate actions. The combination of system and world situation and behavioral sequences leads to the action that should take place. Without understanding the situation it is impossible to make determinations about the sensibility of actions.
- **Inputs** to systems are the only things that can cause effects. Inputs include behaviors that are not available to the machine even though they exist. For example, low-level signals are digitized. Therefore, examining original inputs must be used in some cases to understand what is going on.
- **Outputs** from systems can indicate problems. In many cases, outputs are directly detected as unacceptable. In other cases, different outputs are acceptable in different contexts.
- **State** information is rarely available to analytical systems; however, the state of the machine dictates input processing and the resulting state changes and outputs.
- **Changes** to states are the result of inputs interacting with previous state. Internal behaviors are almost always reflected in state changes. Typically, attacks on systems generate undesirable state changes that produce the undesired side effects.

2.6.1.5   Identity ("Who")

Identity and the management of identity in the world and within systems is commonly considered a fundamental aspect of protection. A basic principle is to take identity, authenticate it to the desired level of surety for the need, and use the identity to authorize access and actions. This allows the protection architecture to work.

■ **Names** are typically associated with all of the identified items of interest, whether they be individuals or things. The design of name spaces is important, among other things, because many things may be identified by systems and name conflicts can cause incorrect system behaviors.

■ **Types** are usually associated with identity information. For example, there may be people, things, and subtypes associated with them.

■ **Properties** are typically associated with named identities. This includes linkage to roles and rules, properties associated with identity for controls of various sorts, information about locations, times, their capabilities to authenticate, biometric properties, and any number of other factors.

■ **Basis** for identity implies that different reasons for associating identity may exist. The differentiation of basis has utility. For example, the assertion of an identity may be associated by way of a federation with a trading partner who provided the information, or it may be associated with a DNA examination tracked to parents. The former is clearly adequate for uses than the latter.

■ **Certainty** is reflected in the application of the basis to validate identity and the need for certainty in the application of that identity. For users from the Internet accessing library records, no certainty is typically required or desired. They may even make up their own identities for that purpose. But for access to financial systems of an enterprise to perform large dollar value electronic funds transfers, far more certainty is desired. Multiple authentications, proper locations at time, proper basis, and other similar factors may be considered in the decision to grant authorization.

2.6.1.6   Method ("How")

How things happen is often used as a means of control and, of course, surety levels and similar facets of protection are inherently tied to the methods used to accomplish them.

■ **Hardware** tends to provide more certainty of function because it is less flexible and less subject to the sorts of design flaws commonly found in software. It is also less complex than software from a standpoint of the sizes of the state machines, it takes longer to create and modify, it can be more thoroughly tested, and it is more expensive to reproduce in low volume.

■ **Software** is the opposite of hardware in the respects described above. It is more flexible, more subject to design flaws of certain sorts, less sure, more complex, easier to create and modify, less throughly tested, and less expensive to reproduce than hardware.

■ **Route** controls are designed to use the path from place to place to increase the level of certainty that content is what it is reported to be. In practice this may be a network path, a physical path, or whatever part of these paths is identifiable by the recipient.

■ **Means** is generally associated with the way something was done and is used in legal parlance associated with patents, which are means and methods for accomplishing some task.

- **Transforms** can seal information and be used to prove to those that can verify the seal or unseal the package that the creator had the transform.
- **Protocols** are used to differentiate request types. Typically, any protocol can be "tunneled" through any data path, and steganographic encoding can be used to supply arbitrary content over any data path while meeting syntactic requirements. Protocols are, nonetheless, used to verify certain properties of communications.
- **Packet or line** are often used to differentiate how content arrives or is sent, and these are often controlled to limit paths.
- **Physicality** is used in certain interfaces, such as the console interface to most systems, to differentiate actions that are allowed. Most systems have limitations on nonconsole access. For example, changing basic input — output system (BIOS) settings can sometimes only be done during the bootstrap process through the console interface.
- **Voice, data, and video** paths are often differentiated so that certain functions can only be performed over certain types of interfaces or with certain types of content. For example, some systems use audio validation processes or perform a challenge with audio information that can only be responded to with data, forcing the user to have proper capabilities and configurations on their systems in order to gain access.

2.6.2 Life Cycles

Life cycles are associated with businesses, systems, people, and data. These life cycles include a wide range of different processes over which protection must be considered in order to have an effective overall protection program.

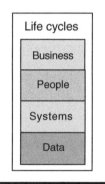

2.6.2.1 Business

Business life cycles have many interactions with information protection programs that are ignored in the literature to a large extent, even though their effects can be dramatic. All business changes have significant impacts on employee behaviors, and there are many cases in which these produce disgruntled employees, layoffs, firings, and organizational changes. These imply significant information protection issues beyond what is listed in the drill-downs here.

- **Formation** of businesses and the processes involved increasingly expose a lot of information to public view. For example, in order to form a corporation and get a bank account in California today, you may have to provide a fingerprint to the bank and personal information to the state to allow them to track you down if they should want to. When businesses are formed there are automatic processes that notify vendors who pay the state for information about the formation and use the data provided under force by the state to contact the owners to sell things to them. When new businesses are formed by existing businesses there may be effects on credit and other similar interactions.

- **Funding** processes involve much detailed financial information, often including credit checks on individuals associated with businesses and containing a wide array of private information. Funding processes are also used to feed data into large databases that are widely accessible for a fee or, in some cases, for free. The funding processes often involve information that can be readily used in identity theft or, in rare cases, business identity theft in which the identity of the business is stolen and used to perpetrate frauds. Funding profiles for businesses often ignore information protection issues and, as a result, the function is ignored in start-up processes to the detriment of the shareholders.

- **Operation** of businesses include the sorts of information protection requirements described throughout the widely published literature.

- **Initial public offerings** (IPOs) lead to the need to run companies as public rather than private entities, and this has dramatic effects on the legal and regulatory requirements in terms of information protection. The basic issue with an IPO is that the value of their investment depends on the integrity, availability, confidentiality, accountability, and use control of the enterprise's information and infrastructure. As a result, it must meet due diligence requirements, be reasonable and prudent, and produce results the CEO can attest to.

- **Joint ventures** and similar business arrangements require special protective measures, particularly when companies compete in other markets. This is necessary in order to prevent (1) collusions or revelation of pricing information, which might violate restraint of trade requirements, (2) competitive information from being leaked, (3) corruption of one enterprise by the other through the joint venture, and (4) other similar negative consequences. However, the participants in the venture must still effectively work together and reach back into their respective infrastructures for day-to-day operations and content relevant to the joint venture and not in the public domain.

- **Mergers and acquisitions** lead to the combination of information technology components, capabilities, and systems, mixing of staff, and exchanges of content that are typically controlled by completely different information protection programs. There is a very significant cost associated with the transition of an entity into a new security operations process. Someone ultimately has to end up in charge, firewalls between entities have to be created so they can interoperate while the protection infrastructures are reconciled, information classifications have to be reconciled in order to gain proper controls, the clearances and need-to-know designations have to be reconciled, interdependencies change, risk aggregations shift, and so forth. This is an effort comparable to the start up of a new protection program in one of the entities and similar to major infrastructure changes in the other. These changes tend to produce disgruntled and laid off employees, and this must also be considered.

- **Divestiture** typically involves the splitting of information and information systems between the two resulting entities. There are many implications for information protection. For example, for every role in each resulting entity, the split has to result in appropriate membership levels. Since those in roles tend to be organizationally bound, critical roles may be moved wholesale into one entity resulting in critical unfulfilled operational roles in the other. There are many solutions to this. Some of these situations involve large business units with their own mirror of the CISO organization, which makes it a lot easier. One of the entities may have to add positions to mirror what the enterprise did for them before divestiture. In a sale to another entity, that entity may have necessary functions already. In other cases, large parts of the IT organization are retained in one entity and its services leased to the other entity for a pre-arranged period of time. This provides for the transition. Typically, these arrangement are for 3 years or more. These changes also tend to produce disgruntled employees and this must also be considered.

- **Bankruptcy** can either be for reorganization or for termination of the existence of the entity. Reorganization is not very significant from a protection standpoint other than the effect of creating disgruntled and frightened employees. Termination of a business leads to termination of all employees and sale of assets. This implies a variety of information protection functions that are usually poorly fulfilled and bring possible liability to the officers. Private information protected by law includes, but it not limited to, protected health information, individual financial information, human resources information like employee records, and business financial records. All of these must be properly stored or disposed of according to the legal requirements for that sort of data. Proprietary materials from third parties, like trade secrets, must be protected. Items covered by intellectual property rights, like copyrighted materials, may have to be protected. Classified or similarly controlled information has to be properly handled regardless of the business status of the entity. In short, end-of-life processes must be properly managed during a bankruptcy process.
- **Dissolution** for any other reason than bankruptcy, or at the end of the bankruptcy process, also has to deal with the life cycle issues associated with systems, data, and people.

2.6.2.2 People

People have life cycles and every facet of their life has implications for the enterprise and its information protection program. From before conception to long after burial, there are life cycle issues in the enterprise.

- **Conception** is typically a private matter; however, prior to conception, health care programs at the enterprise have to reflect proper status of the mother in order to assure that medical care and job assignments are proper for the status of the individual. Women of child-bearing age are restricted from certain roles for liability reasons. These issues are handled by information systems and must be properly protected from disclosure or corruption while still being reflected in roles available to the individuals in use control processes.

- **Pregnancy** usually brings more use restrictions and changes behavioral patterns of individuals. This leads to differences in behavioral detection models and responses to different sorts of behavioral detection results. Work hours may change, location may change, and in the latter stages, leaves may start, with the corresponding change in use control.

- **Birth** creates new identities within enterprise systems, for example, associated with health care programs and in similar areas. These identities have different status than others within the enterprise records and require different protections.

- **Education** impacts qualifications of employees for different positions and benefits are often associated with education. For children of employees, school and day care records may be available at the company for emergency contact or other purposes. These have special protection requirements as well because they may involve protection of minors.

- **Marriage** often brings about name changes that need to be reflected in identity records, but these changes require historic association in order for time to be properly accounted for. Most current identity management systems handle such changes poorly. Marriage also has impacts on benefits and other similar issues that lead to the need to protect different information in different ways. Marriage changes behaviors, and the protection system must compensate for these changes as well.

- **Divorce**, like marriage, often brings about name changes, requires tracking processes, changes of status, benefits, and other information, and has implications for privacy of records. Divorce is also a life change that may produce erratic behaviors. It tends to remove stabilizing factors that effect suitability for certain tasks, however, these effects are not universal. As a result, it needs to trigger an evaluation relative to life stability for people in sensitive positions.

- **Training** and the tracking of training is important to the protection program because it affects qualifications and because training requirements associated with certain job functions must be fulfilled in a timely fashion or the individual has to be decertified for those tasks.

- **Hiring** processes involve background checks, verification of resume facts, and checking of references. These are important to initial establishment of clearances at hiring. For sensitive positions, more in-depth checks are required. In the information protection program, such checks are typically made part of the personnel reliability program. Hiring processes also involve requirements for initial awareness and training that must be fulfilled and documented, creation of new enterprise identity information, association of roles with individuals, and other similar processes associated with granting access to enterprise systems and the initiation of behavior and life cycle tracking processes.

- **Promotion** typically comes with new responsibilities associated with information protection. The training and awareness program needs to include new security-related duties in the promotion process, including issues associated with the evaluation of security performance in subordinates, where appropriate. Promotion may result in changes in authorized access, and this has to be reflected in role changes and access to systems, facilities, and information. Behavioral changes associated with the new position have to be reflected in detection profiles. Promotion also requires a process for hand-off of content and capabilities to replacements as appropriate.

- **Demotion** is usually not a happy moment in a career, and it is a time of change that can often generate a disgruntled employee. Behavioral changes must be watched as well as recalibrated for the new roles and responsibilities. Demotion typically results in role and access changes and these are typically supposed to happen during the meeting when the employee is notified of the change. Demotion also requires a process for hand-off of content and capabilities to replacements as appropriate.

- **Suspension** mandates the suspension of many but not all information technology privileges for the period of the suspension, tends to generate disgruntled employees, and results in behavioral changes that need to be reflected in behavior tracking systems. This also requires a process for hand-off of content and capabilities to replacements.

- **Vacation** should lead to temporary suspension of many but not all employee information technology privileges for the period of the vacation. Vacations tend to lead to short-term changes in employee behavior upon return, but these end in a day or two in most cases. Training and awareness levels should be checked on return. A process for hand-off of content and capabilities to replacements may be needed.

- **Illness** severe enough to produce days away should generate changes in information system access for the period of the illness.

- **Leaves** typically run for periods of days, weeks, months, or more and should be associated with temporary suspension of many but not all information system access. Upon return from a leave, training and awareness typically has to be undertaken to catch the individual up to the current situation, and this includes updated security awareness and recertification on systems where the training requirements may have lapsed. Extended leaves also requires a process for hand-off of content and capabilities to replacements as appropriate and return of the hand-offs upon return.

- **Job changes** produce changed roles in most cases, resulting in the need to terminate previous accounts, create new ones, and so forth. This also requires a process for hand-off of content and capabilities to replacements as appropriate.

- **Moves** involving home address changes or changes in workplace or office number lead to changes in access controls associated with network connections, and other similar changes within systems and tracking. Updates to historic records to reflect these changes are needed in order to assure that mail gets redirected, and movement of content and systems from place to place require physical protection during the move. Inventory processes should be undertaken before and after such moves to assure that lost items of value are identified and that loss is prevented where possible. Moves often result in end of life processes for stored data and this has to be properly handled as well.

- **Resignation** typically involves a planned departure. The circumstances may dictate special precautions, and because resignations, unlike terminations, are not surprises, there are typically concerns about theft of proprietary information between the notice and the termination of duties. As soon as the company is notified of a resignation, information protection actions need to be taken to protect against actions of the terminal employee, and sensitive access should be removed or closely surveilled for the duration of employment. Most resignations are given on a few weeks notice which provides time for transfer of content and knowledge; however, content should be immediately secured to the extent it is in tangible form to assure against any actions by a disgruntled employee who may be resigning. A standard resignation process should be in place to manage this process properly. Many resignations correspond to competitive moves and these should be examined if potential harm could result.

- **Termination** typically involves a formal meeting in which the employee is notified of the termination. During this meeting systems access should be suspended or terminated, all equipment and access devices should be gathered, and proper forms should be signed to acknowledge termination requirements and reaffirm employee agreement issues. Information technology should preserve data associated with the individual at this time and provide means for administrative access. The employee should be escorted from the moment of the start of the termination meeting until they leave the premises. If they need to clean out their desk, this should be supervised by an adequately knowledgeable person to assure that only authorized material is removed. This process should be well defined and consistently applied at all levels. Home access should also be terminated and any equipment or other materials in their home should be gathered as part of the termination process. A common practice is to withhold the last paycheck until extant material like badges and equipment is returned in good condition.

- **Retirement** is usually a ceremonial time with a party and memories of various sorts displayed for fellow employees. From an information protection standpoint it is very much like any other termination. The process should be similar, well defined, and strictly followed.

- **Death** of a worker may seem like the end of the life cycle tracking but it is not. It is processed similar to a termination except that the employee is unavailable for participation in the process. If there is a death in the worker's family rather than the worker, the life change will result in some behavioral changes as well as th need to invoke processes associated with insurance and so forth.

- **Legacy** of employees, even after termination or death, continues for a substantial period. Records have to be retained for different time periods depending on specifics, but normally 7 years of history are retained for business records unless other requirements apply. Accounts and data may be used over a long time frame and these should be reassigned to those who take over the workload. The identity information associated with an employee may remain associated with their identity and data life cycle processes must be careful not to mis-associate identity with legacy information. Retirement funds and other similar financial or health-related information may continue to be handled for a long period of time, and benefits may accrue to dependents and descendants indefinitely.

2.6.2.2.1   Disgruntled Employees and Ex-Employees

There are really only three choices to dealing with those who are not happy with the company: (1) terminate their employment, (2) make them happier with work, or (3) let them fester and eventually cause harm. Making them happy is preferred if they are highly productive. If this fails or they are marginal, termination is preferred. Festering is undesirable for all but often done. Ex-employees without access predominantly threaten leaks and harassment and must be met with court orders and similar mechanisms when they get hostile.

2.6.2.3   *Systems*

Systems have life cycles that can be as short as a few weeks or months to as long as decades. Hardware replacement cycles typically dictate that components are replaced within 10 years of installation for most computer systems, but some supporting infrastructure equipment like telephony systems and cabling, air conditioning, and heating units last for 30 or 40 years. And many systems have all of their hardware and software replaced over time in an evolutionary process. As a rule of thumb, changes in systems have costs that increase by a factor of 3 to 10 for each step in the life cycle up to maintenance. So every poor protection-related decision made early that could have been changed for a dollar in the conceptual phase of the system results in repair costs in the range of hundreds of thousands to millions of dollars in operation.

- The **concept** for a system typically comes from a few people who think up the idea of what the system will do. This is the point where considerations about information protection should start to enter the picture. The protection concept should be an inherent component of the idea underlying the effort. This is more important for bigger ideas that will have longer life cycles because the errors made early will turn into larger and larger costs over the life cycle.
- **Design** of systems must consider information protection issues in order to make choices that lead down more fruitful, more securable, and less costly paths in the long run. Designers should consider all of the life cycle areas as well as the need for integrity, availability, confidentiality, use control, and accountability. They also need to have adequate expertise to make reasonably good design decisions with regard to these issues, and this requires adequate background and education in these specialty areas that is largely lacking in most engineering and computer backgrounds today.
- **Engineering** systems to work within an environment often involves a lot of systems integration. In this effort there are many sources of incompatibilities between systems that have to be resolved in order to allow interoperability. These interface issues are also security issues in most modern systems. In many cases the engineering design has faults that are carried into implementation because the problems were not thought through as deeply as they should be. As there is no systematic approach

to engineering solutions, it is the creativity of the engineers that has to be counted on. A large part of the engineering experience is related to what the engineers have seen before, so it is important that they be exposed to many of the more common security-related design faults in order to avoid them in their designs. There are also some limited tools that help check designs for known fault types. Design processes associated with high quality are typically applicable, and the CMM-SEC and NSTSSI processes are important to doing a reasonably secure design.

- **Implementation** involves security issues associated with procurement of components, design and code review processes, protection testing, audits, change control processes for the larger environment, and so forth. Implementation has to integrate system audit with enterprise audit and enterprise control into system control. Integration of intrusion detection and response systems, identity management, zoning policies, and other similar protection measures into systems happens at this time and, of course, it had better have been considered in the earlier phases.

- **Operation** of systems involves all of the enterprise protection processes and has to produce metrics, generate audit trails, take control signals, fail in a safe mode for the rest of its environment, remain within control requirements, and perform useful tasks efficiently.

- **Maintenance** processes introduce many opportunities for attack, often including remote maintenance or similar capabilities that bypass other protective barriers and controls. These require special maintenance modes and controls, including separation from other systems while in maintenance, sound change control processes for making changes, and verification and reintegration after maintenance. Maintenance periods typically involve different people than normal operation periods. Proper control over their presence and access has to be maintained. Storage media used in maintenance have to be protected as does data associated with testing processes and special access and passwords associated with maintenance processes. Maintenance access should be disabled during normal operating periods.

- **Disasters** occur from a wide range of causes and with enough frequency and range of effect that they destroy or disable components of systems within significant radii. Overall business function for substantial businesses has to survive disasters that leave most of its potential business operating, but not global catastrophes that would put it out of business regardless of information technology. This can only be done by redundancy in capabilities, people, and diversity of locations. During disasters, normal physical protections in place will almost certainly fail, but the overall protection, in terms of risk management requirements, must not fail, even at this time. Planning must include the potential for disasters.

- **Recovery** processes involve the ability to restore business operations in a timely fashion after a disaster. This requires people, systems, data, and business change-overs, and a well-tested and practiced plan. Recovery should have well-defined starting and ending conditions and process checks along the way. During recovery, normal protective measures are often bypassed. Risk management should either dictate that the change in risk profiles be acceptable or otherwise mitigate these increased risks as part of the recovery process.

■ **Upgrades** to systems are commonly done without significant concern about protection; however, for medium and high valued systems, change control processes should be required. These processes assure that upgrades are thoroughly tested before being put into use. Testing normally covers operation over a period of time under benign circumstances. Protection testing for malicious attacks is a far different challenge. Malicious upgrades have been used by attackers, so verifying the source and integrity of the upgrade is vital to effective change control. Change control over systems changes is often not feasible at the level desired, and at some point risk has to be accepted in most cases. As the value of the system increases, acceptance of risk should be made harder and harder.

■ **Transformations** of systems from function to function tend to happen over time. Transformations are typically evolutionary and, when not properly planned, they often result in protection issues. As a general rule, planning these changes start at the conceptual level and working through all of the other early systems phases is an effective way to deal with transformations.

■ **Consolidation** of systems to join functions is a common cost saving activity, but as systems are consolidated, the risks associated with the preconsolidation systems are aggregated into the consolidated result. The resulting risk aggregation has to be analyzed and proper safeguards taken to compensate for the change in risk and resulting change in requirement for certainty associated with the result.

■ **Obsolescence** happens as systems near the end of their useful life cycle. As systems enter this phase of operation they are generally replaced or a decision is made to terminate the functions they provide. Over time the maintenance costs go up until it is more cost effective to recreate the system than to run it any longer. During this phase of operation there is a tendency to reduce the utility of the system and its criticality, thus reducing it protection requirements. The key thing to assure here is that the protection is reduced only as the risk is reduced.

■ **End-of-life** happens for all systems eventually. As systems become decommissioned, care must be taken to assure that they are no longer needed. This typically involves running at least one full business cycle of every function of the system still desired before shutting the old system down. After the system is shut down, residual data remains an issue from a confidentiality standpoint, and accountability remains an issue until all value is certified as gone. Formal policy, procedures, standards, and documentation are required for system end-of-life.

■ **Reconstitution** of systems after the end of their life cycle is rare but it can and sometimes does happen. In this case, all of the protective functions associated with its creation must be followed and reviewed for changes in situation between the time the system was decommissioned and when it will be reconstituted. After reconstitution, normal processes associated with end-of-life must be redone when the system is again decommissioned.

■ **Resale** of systems after decommissioning should be straight forward. The only real requirements are verification of the decommissioning process and its resulting elimination of residual data and value, and documentation associated with the accountability aspects of the sale.

- **Destruction** of systems, once data has been removed is used for cases where the junk value of the components resulting from destruction exceeds the resale value of the system or where disposal is less expensive than alternatives. Destruction can also happen as a result of events. If destruction is for resale value or disposal, end-of-life processes should assure that residual value is appropriate and destruction may proceed following all applicable laws and regulations associated with environmental and health standards. Many computer systems include parts with hazardous chemicals, such as PCBs, and care must be taken in disposal to avoid downstream liability. For systems destroyed as a result of events, additional end-of-life processes may be required to assure that residual value such as confidential data is not present in the destroyed form.

- **Recycling** of components and materials is fairly common in the computer industry, and it should be considered as an alternative to destruction and disposal. One of the best programs is the use of old computer equipment in schools, where 3–5-year-old personal computers may be well-used for many years. Recycling of materials within systems, such as gold, silver, and other metals, can often pay for the destruction and disposal process associated with the remaining components. Many companies now put used computers up for sale on eBay or other auction sites. They may only get ten cents on the dollar, but this is ten cents they didn't have before, and they avoid the expense of proper disposal. If fully depreciated, income may need to be balanced against disposal costs. Finally, computer museums are starting to arise, so old high-valued systems may be turned into museum pieces at the end of their life.

2.6.2.4   Data

Life cycles for data are often ignored because data is thought of as passive; however, data is the representation of the content that is vital to business operations. Throughout its life cycle, data must be properly cared for to assure that the business operates as it should. The terms data, information, knowledge, and wisdom are often intertwined and misused. Generally, data as presented here is the representation of content (the stuff that has utility). Information is defined as symbolic representations in any form. Knowledge is something that computers don't really have, but if they were to be considered in this light, knowledge would likely be regarded as the combination of information and processing suited to applying it to useful purposes. Wisdom is rarely found in people and certainly never found in computers except as data representing human wisdom, if properly interpreted.

- **Inception** of data occurs when real-world events take place outside of the realm of the computer system or when the computer generates some internal signals at an electromagnetic, optical, mechanical, or other physical level. All sorts of data exists that cannot be sensed by computers, and this is ignored by the computers leading to limitations on their cognitive input capacity.

- **Observation** depends on the sensor capabilities and limits of the device doing the sensing, and the ability of the system reading that sensory data to interpret it and transform it into a form that it can use. For example, many programs read inputs and ignore certain characters, and systems typically strip off protocol elements in the receipt of data. The limits of observation are also limits on the ability of the system to differentiate inputs of different sorts and a resulting loss of capacity to detect many deviations that could yield useful information about source and integrity.

- **Entry** is generally considered the time at which the data becomes something that can be stored, used, processed, output, or otherwise comes into the control and possession of the computer system at the logical level of programs being able to act on it.

- **Validation** processes are often used to check for proper syntax, limits, and internal consistency. Syntax checks are fundamental to effective security and failure to do proper syntax checks at input is responsible for the vast majority of current technical computer attacks. Generally, no input sequence that is not legitimate and valid for the application in context should be accepted. This includes limits on length, value, symbols, and symbol sequences, and all of these in the context of program state. Limits are used to prevent excesses based on policies or design. For example, input length limits should correspond to designed storage for inputs, and dollar value limits on transaction amounts should be determined by user, context, and company policies. Many inputs contain redundancy, such as the entry of a postal code and state in a form. As many postal codes map to one state, any sort of inconsistency between an entered postal code and the entered state can lead to a detection of invalid input. Addresses can often be tracked to zip codes today because of the increasing accuracy of geographic data, so these checks can be very effective at correcting input errors as soon as possible.

- **Verification** is the use of redundancy to confirm or refute assumptions. For most cases, verification implies a separate and different method of confirmation than the original source. For example, if the weather report indicates high humidity, it can be readily verified by a sensor. The level of verification typically depends on costs associated with verification and risks associated with the use of unverified data.

- **Attribution** associates data to its source. Generally, there are four levels of attribution discussed in the literature. Level 1 attribution is associated with the physical input channel, such as the remote IP address, the wire that the signal arrived on, the telephone number of the remote data entry terminal, or the terminal connector that was used for the entry. Level 2 attribution seeks the indirect version of level 1 attribution, attempting to track data to the system or hardware device that transmitted it. Level 3 attribution, also known as source attribution, associates data with its human source, the individual responsible for its entry. Level 4 attribution associates data with the organization behind its source. Level 1 is usually relatively easy. Level 2 is very complicated unless a great deal of surveillance is in place. Level 3 depends on psychological characteristics and may be easier than level 2 if differentiation of source rather then specific identity is desired. Level 4 attribution requires an intelligence operation to be effective in a malicious environment. Attribution and the ability to verify attribution leads to assessment of trust. For example, when a well known expert says a product is good, it may be taken far more seriously than when an anonymous reviewer on eBay says it is good.

■ **Fusion** of data takes place in systems that typically do normalization and correlation of some sort. The result is typified by proximity to known situations in a state space. This produces secondary, tertiary, and n-ary derivative information that is applied or stored as data for other processes. Fusion is fraught with errors and assumptions and is thus a far more complex issue from a protection standpoint than data. Fused data also has mixes of the properties associated with the sources and processing mechanisms used to derive it. For example, if highly sensitive data like the schedule of a military operation is fused with common data, like weather information, the result may be highly sensitive (i.e., the change in schedule due to a storm) or far less sensitive (i.e., the total fuel consumption estimates for the operation which may vary because of weather, time, target location or other factors). Fusion leads to data aggregation as well, and this can cause two otherwise nonsensitive pieces of information to be sensitive when combined. For example, departmental total salary may not be sensitive while individual salary might be. But if you can get departmental totals before and after each new employee is hired into the department, you can readily derive the starting salary of each individual. Similarly, because of the nature of pricing of medical procedures and tests, knowing the medical fees paid leads to the procedures and tests performed, which in turn leads to the medical conditions of the patients. Thus, medical bills become sensitive, protected health information because of the ability to fuse them into protected health information.

■ **Separation** requirements associated with data are generated because only separation technologies are sure to limit the flow of data. Data separation is typically at the heart of zoning policies and other related issues. Generally, data is associated with classifications and users are associated with clearances. Data is only accessible to users when the user clearance is commensurate with the data classification. Functions performed are then limited based on the needs of the user with respect to the data.

■ **Analysis** of data involves the processing of the data through state machines so that the output of the state machine has utility in a different context. This is typically the sort of thing done when so-called raw data is mixed with other data, transforms, and process models to produce meaningful content for the user that is only indirectly related to the data itself. For example, temperature gradients on a wing may be mixed with simulation models and analyzed to determine aircraft stability. Errors in analysis may produce dramatic side effects, so the integrity of the analysis process is often critical to the business function. For example, analysis of data associated with a bridge may reveal or fail to reveal structural limitations that could cause the bridge to fail under load conditions.

■ **Transforms** are commonly used to change data media, representation, form, format, or utility. For example, data associated with a simulation may be transformed into graphical format and mapped into a picture to produce a graphic depiction of an event. Transforms are commonly used to extract subsets of data — for example, to differentiate intrusion-related audit data from unrelated data. Transforms are used to change data into formats used in different applications or systems, like a transform from EBCDIC to ASCII for moving content from mainframes to personal computers. Transforms are used to reformat data, such as putting a presentation into columns. Transforms are used to change media — for example, to place the data on a backup tape. All of these transforms are critical to the function they support and thus integrity must be protected for business function to be protected.

- **Transmission** is generally associated with the data in motion state as described elsewhere. In transmission, data becomes susceptible to a larger set of attacks associated with the larger physical space and increased number of media and systems it passes through, or comes into contact with.

- **Storage** is generally associated with the data at rest state which is described elsewhere. In storage, data tends to be localized and concentrated in a small physical space, and thus has the advantage of being physically securable and the disadvantage of aggregating risk.

- **Use** of data is generally associated with the data in use state described elsewhere. When in use, data must be in usable form. There are few options for protection of the data without protection of the mechanism that uses it. Thus, protection of data in use typically involves protection of the operating environment using it.

- **Presentation** of data typically involves transformation into a presentation format and display on an output device. This may be presentation for human consumption or for automation such as process control systems. It is critical that the presentation accurately represent the intent of the application. For example, many presentations are intentionally deceptive, or at least misleading in that they emphasize things the presenter wants to put forth and minimize issues the presenter wants to be ignored. The presentation of statistical information is notorious enough to have its own saying: "There are lies, damned lies, and statistics." From an information protection standpoint, this has a range of implications.

- **Modification** of data can be accidental, intentional and appropriate, or malicious. Accidental modification is generally undesirable and can be covered by relatively simple statistically verifiable controls such as redundancy and fault tolerance. Intentional and appropriate modification is desirable from the standpoint of being able to enter and alter values associated with the business utility of the system. For example, changing your address so you can continue to get your mail when you change offices is a business function that involves legitimate alteration of address data. Malicious modification of data is highly undesirable and protection typically involves the use of cryptographic checksums for detection and access controls for prevention. Someone else changing your address as part of an identity theft is an example of the same change used for a malicious purpose. Integrity is a function of intent, and computers are notoriously bad at dealing with issues of intent.

- **Loss** of data can cause business consequences associated with the value of the data unless appropriate protections are in place. Value comes in the form of business utility associated with its use. That utility may be lost from the loss of data. Redundancy protects against loss of utility unless all redundant copies are also lost or unavailable in a suitable time frame for use. Preventing release depends on confidentiality protections, typically mandating the use of encryption or prevention from physical access, even when in possession of the data's container.

- **Recovery** of lost data comes in one of several forms. The data may be backed up or otherwise kept, sent, or created redundantly; it may be regeneratable at a cost, it may be recoverable from partially broken or deleted media, and it may be located and recovered by physical or electronic means. Insurance may cover the value, and the legal process may aid in recovery of the value through civil and/or criminal actions. With the exception of risk transfer techniques, these typically involve outside specialized expertise associated with data recovery, computer forensics, private investigative, or law enforcement processes.

- **Reconstruction** of data is sometimes a choice if the data is derived from other data that is available, if fragments exist at different places, or if the original values can be derived from other data values associated with or derived from it. A really good example was a data set that was destroyed in a fire but was reconstructed from portions of it that were previously emailed to other parties. Those parties sent back copies of partial subsets, and they were combined together to reconstruct enough of the original data to meet the need.

- **Backup** of data is a fundamental process designed to assure availability over time. Different sorts of backup are required for different circumstances. The decision about which types to apply stem from timeliness, redundancy, transportation, quantity, and duration issues. For data that has to be restored from backups in near real time, duplicate (hot standby) systems are typically used. For data that has to be very redundant, the redundancy requirement leads to the number of copies and their diversity in space and media. For data in large quantity or that has to be at distant locations in some time frame, different media and bandwidth are acceptable. For backups required to last different amounts of time, different storage media and processes are used. All of these vary with the specifics of the application, almost all combinations of these are attainable, and the costs vary with the need. More and harsher requirements both increase costs. For typical data, typical backup regimens include daily incremental backup of changed data that day and that are kept for one week, weekly incremental or full backups of all data that are kept for a month, monthly full backups that are kept for a year, and annual full backups that are kept indefinitely or retained for the legally mandated duration for business records. Backups have to be tested by restoration on a regular basis in order to assure that they work, tracking backups and selectively restoring from them is problematic for sequential media such as tapes, and large-scale backup facilities on-site and off-site are commonly used for data centers.

- **Restoration** from backups is a process that its typically tuned to the backup process. Restoration processes depend to a large extent on timeliness requirements and media. Restoration in real-time usually requires backups on media similar to the original, and in many cases is implemented by transaction replay processes at secondary sites. Less real-time restoration can involve wider ranges of processes.

■ **Destruction** of data is problematic. Generally there are several types of destruction processes associated with digital data and different methods associated with paper, CD-ROM, DVD, and fiche data that are most commonly used.

   ■ For digital data stored on disk or tape, deletion of files is most common and least effective. It is trivial to restore this data, and it should never be used to destroy data of substantial value. Secure deletion based on multiple pattern-based overwrites is used against medium-grade threats. For higher grade threats electromagnetic erasure with high Oersted field generators can be used but is limited because generators may inadequately penetrate the media. Physical mangling of disks is ineffective against high-grade threats because remaining fragments store large quantities of data per unit area. Destruction of media and contents by burning at high temperatures or boiling in acid for long enough time is most effective.

   ■ For paper media, strip shredders are the most common method of destruction. They are ineffective, and easily and consistently defeated, leaving only a false sense of security. Cross-cut shredders are more secure but to be reasonably safe, shreds should be sized on the order of a few square millimeters for typical printouts. Sensitive and nonsensitive data should be joined in the shred bins to increase volumes. Shredding should be done by the individual doing the disposal, not through a service that shreds elsewhere. The best common process cross-cut shreds, then burns or pulps in a recycling process physically controlled by cleared personnel.

   ■ For CD-ROMs and fiche, data density is far higher than for paper. Shredders of the sort described above are effective but leave shreds large enough to extract useful content. Burning or emulsification with acid is preferred.

2.6.3 Protection Process: Data State

Data is generally treated differently when at rest, in motion, and in use, and the data state has a great deal to do with the protection mechanisms and need for protection. There is an age-old characterization of data at rest, in motion, and in use, but today, with mobile computing, data is often at rest in a disk and in motion because the disk is in a personal data assistant or laptop computer. Or it may be in motion because the laptop is on an airplane and in use. So in a sense we have a new state of data. But tapes were always moved from

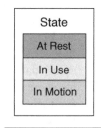

site to site as part of backups, and airplanes have had computers in them ever since computers came into substantial use. So when these terms are used, they refer to properties of the data. More than one set of properties may be in effect at any given time.

2.6.3.1 Data at Rest

Data at rest is, in essence, data stored at a physical location in a physical device, typically a disk, CD, USB storage device, etc. In most cases, computers with high valued information in large quantities remain in one physical location. This means that the physical security measures associated with that location act as a significant part of the protection afforded to that data.

- **Storage** of data is in physical devices like disks, tapes, CD-ROMs, DVDs, paper, fiche, and more recently electronic storage devices like PCMCIA cards, USB drives, etc.
  - **Tapes** are usually disconnected from any computing device and only come in contact with those devices when passing by the tape head that reads or writes them. They are often manipulated using robotic devices to move them between large storage areas and tape readers and writers. Those readers and writers are most often disconnected from the computers that use them, and they are accessed at a distance over internal cabling. Tapes are large enough that they have to be concealed with something else that is noticeable in order to be removed, often have bar codes or other similar markings to allow them to be identified and tracked, and are usually stored within hardened data centers and other similar areas. It takes much time to go through a tape, and it can really only be accessed sequentially, so while it can have a high burst rate, it is slow to get to any particular place in a tape, and it takes as much time to delete a whole tape as it does to write over it all. Because of the large numbers of tapes compared to drives in a typical data center, it would take weeks or months to erase a large percentage of the data. Tapes are rarely missed over periods of hours to days so they can often be removed, read or written, replaced, and not missed. Tapes need to be read every few years in order to be refreshed; as they age beyond 10 years they start to become unusable, and they tend to lose data when placed into environments in excess of 100°F. RFID tags are usable on tapes and may be applied in some circumstances to track movement into and out of facilities and areas.
  - **Disks** are high speed for input and output, typically sized either for laptops (about 3 in. × 2 in. × π in.) or for internal use (about 2 in. × 3.5 in. × 6 in.). They store up to about 250 GB each, can read, write, or delete information at about 4 GB/min, are randomly accessible for rapid access to files, include the electronics needed to read and write them, and are usually stored in systems that are using them all the time. Additionally, they are generally in use, it is hard to remove them for duplication or destruction without being noticed additionally, they are usually within cases inside systems, it is often hard to gain physical access without being quite obvious. Disks are usually replaced every 3–5 years because storage is increasing so quickly that 100 5-year-old

disks can be replaced by one new disk. They also tend to fail after 2–3 years of use, so replacement is mandatory to reliability. Old disks lose value quickly, so they are often discarded instead of being resold. Proper destruction is critical to the protection process, and these disks must be properly handled.

- **Paper** storage is one of the most overlooked security issues in many modern enterprises. In almost every protection-posture assessment, paper-based data that is readily accessible contains enormously damaging information that nobody notices moving from place to place, can be easily copied, can be burned in a fire, can be used for illegal purposes, and can be altered or replaced unnoticed. In one recent assessment, paper found at one location included (1) hundreds of completed immigration and foreign worker forms; (2) name, address, medical, pay rate, bank account, and Social Security numbers for almost all employees; (3) a complete printout of not-yet-released corporate books for a year including details of customers, suppliers, prices, expenses, locations, and operations; and (4) medical records for thousands of employees. Protection of paper records is clearly vital.

- **Fiche** and similar records are kept in most cases to allow smaller space to be used to store more historical data that must be retained but is rarely accessed. Fiche is far more easily taken without being noticed, can be taken in larger volume because of the smaller size per datum than paper, will almost never be noticed for a long time, and is rarely inventoried, even in the disposal process, to assure that everything that should be disposed of is disposed of.

- **Electronic storage devices** today tend to be relatively small, certainly fitting into a shirt pocket, and in some cases embedded in other small devices. They are readily disguised, operate at high speed, and can tolerate substantial harsh handling without losing data. They attach to a system in a second, are recognized and mounted, can be loaded with data within a few minutes or less, and removed immediately. As a result, they are ideal for moving data in and out of environments surreptitiously. They store on the order of a gigabyte of information, so for most applications, especially espionage, they are very handy. But for corporate storage of high-valued data they are too easily removed, copied, and replaced, too easily stolen, not as reliable as they might be, and harder to control as inventory items or as authoritative sources of data and value.

- **Retaining stored data** requires media-specific processes to assure operation over long time frames. This is typically handled by the automation in those systems. But there are other retention requirements associated with stored data that is far harder to properly carry out. These are the legal requirements for data retention associated with business records and the requirements associated with data retention policy that have to be implemented in information systems. Generally, laws require retention of normal business records for 3, 4, or 7 years in the United States, depending on the specifics, and for material records associated with a business, 7 years' retention are required in the United States, according to Sarbanes-Oxley regulations. Businesses tend to want to eliminate records as soon as possible in order to limit liability, so many have very short retention times for things like email. But this is potentially problematic and may result in fines or criminal sanctions against individuals and companies. EU regulations further complicate issues by requiring that certain privacy-related data not be retained past the amount of time required for its use. For most cases this is something like 7 days to one month for things like passport numbers, telephone numbers, addresses, and so forth. This potentially interferes with customer service requirements, warranty information, shipping and receiving records, and so forth. This also has interactions with backup policies and practices as retention on backups and other media have to be handled. Tracking all of the data at rest also becomes problematic, particularly when it is in motion between being at rest. Even eliminating all records of a particular transaction that is not kept in many records systems becomes difficult. For example, in a recent criminal case all but one copy of a document was removed from records and backups, but one backup copy of a file server copy of the record stored while in transit in an email server ended up being found, and the case was dramatically impacted as a result.

- **Protection of data** at rest is often facilitated by operating system access controls, which can be highly effective. They are often more effective than alternatives. They are faster, more reliable, and better for survivability and recovery processes. They are easier to use than alternatives like disk, file, or record encryption and cryptographic checksums, respectively, for achieving confidentiality, use control, and integrity. Availability is generally assured with redundant disk storage as a local solution and distributed backups, checkpoints, and transaction records as a solution for transaction systems, databases, and file systems that support this sort of change mechanism. Accountability is typically retained by ownership records and accounting data sent to external audit collection and retention systems, retained locally if adequate system protection is available, or sent to Write-Once Read-Many (WORM) disks if they are available for this purpose.

- **Backup** is described elsewhere as associated with data life cycles. Backup for data at rest typically comes in the form of redundant arrays of independent disks (RAID), removable backup media, file server backup areas, transaction-based remote system backups in hot, warm, or cold standby modes, or long-term storage in other forms at remote backup facilities and recovery sites. For most enterprise data centers, backups go to tapes and copies of those backups are sent to a remote site for disaster recovery. Depending on timeliness requirements, backups may be made continuously, periodically, or on special occasions. Backup scheduling is covered under life cycle issues associated with data under backups.

  - **RAID** backups come in the form of multiple disks containing portions of the data in an arrangement that assures that as long as m-out-of-n disks are working, the data will continue to be available in real-time. However, most RAID implementations are designed so that once the (n-m)th disk fails, the data is unavailable and very hard to recover. This makes RAID resilient up to a point and then brittle. Worse yet, because most RAID arrays are implemented with identical disks, there is a tendency for them to be installed together and fail at very nearly the same time. RAID failures out of line with the expectation based on statistics occur because these models ignore the change in failure rates over the life of a device. The so-called bathtub curve indicates that at the start and end of life cycles, failure rates are far higher than the steady state rates during normal operation.

- **Removable media** backups typically include CD-ROMs, DVDs, WORM drives, and tapes; however, increasingly disks are being used in this capacity as well, through removable drive bays and firewire or similar interfaces. Of these choices, for enterprises, only tapes are realistic today in large data centers. Disks are expensive, and no automation exists for storing large numbers of them and automatically mounting and unmounting them. CD-ROMs and DVDs store too little for effective backups of today's large storage media, and inadequate automation for them is also an issue. WORM drives are really only used for specific applications where each operation is backed up for safety or liability reasons, such as in manufacturing facilities. Tapes, with all of their limitations, remain the only real viable removable media for large data center backups.

- **File server backups** are particularly useful for network-based backup approaches. Terabyte (1000 Gigabyte) file servers are now available for about $1000 each. They can be placed on Gigabit or slower Ethernets and used to store backup data from large numbers of systems remotely. Because they are on live systems, restoration can be immediately done by the user who owns the files by copying those files back. Automation is used to backup changed files to these file servers at any desired period, and typically backups happen at the early hours of the morning or at randomly chosen times after network access is available. The scheduling issues are complex here. Backups done when computers are turned on result in large numbers of backups the first thing in the morning, which collapses network availability. Backups scheduled at a time of day fail because the computers are not always on at that time. Backups done by user fail because users fail to remember or do them. Some companies try policies of keeping computers turned on at night; others automate some sort of overnight startup and shut down process, and others try other methods, but all of them have problems. File servers are also useful for backing up larger permanent systems. Storage area networks are the evolution of these file server approaches. They use a name space to provide very large amounts of storage for backup purposes, sometimes ranging into the 1,000 terabyte scale. But even then, care in what is backed up is required to prevent overrunning available capacity. For example, a company with 100,000 computers, each with a 40-gigabyte disk drive that is half used, generate 2,000 terabytes in a single full backup. The vast majority of this data comes from almost identical contents such as operating systems, standard applications, and files that are not very important. The enterprise data classification scheme should include information on what needs to be backed up with what level of redundancy and how often, so that this classification can be used to make automated backup determinations. These backups have another problem in that they typically generate more files and space over time because they intentionally do not delete things that fail to appear on the new backups. If files are moved or copied, the copies are generated and the subsequent deleted copies do not get removed. Tracking the precise file system state for this sort of backup mechanism is not implemented effectively yet today.

- **Transaction-based remote backups** depend on having a transaction system, a transaction-based file system, or another way of turning changes in data at rest into transactions. The initial state is synchronized and then transactions are sent to the remote system and replayed there for updates. As a result, the backup has an identical state to the original. Of course, this has its problems as well. One of the problems is that an attacker who does a massive deletion of files will generate transactions that delete those files on the backup system. For this reason it is important that instead of replaying all transactions as they happen, checkpoints are taken and transactions are recorded. In this way any previous state can be restored. But this process involves even more storage because duplicative efforts generate excess transactions. Nevertheless, this capability is very handy and highly desirable if a proper file system state is to be restored and counters to common attacks are to be successful.

- **Long-term backups** in remote backup facilities and recovery sites are also very common practice. Typically, for disaster recovery purposes, off-site backup copies of tapes or other media are made and physically transported to a backup site for use in an emergency. This is rarely done more than daily because of the limits of the transportation system as opposed to the communications system that is more real-time but lower volume per time (1,000 terabytes can be shipped anywhere in the world in less than a day; however, via communications, this is problematic). Increasingly, remote backup sites allow transaction-based updates or backups, so disaster recovery processes are implemented by doing electronic off-site backups, but the cost of maintaining high-speed lines for this purpose is substantial, and the potential for a remote attack on the off-site backups is also worth considering in an evaluation of the trade offs.

- **Restoration** processes depend on timeliness requirements and backup approach. For real-time restoration, hot standby systems are the only realistic solution. Warm standby systems work for near-real-time restoration, assuming that some amount of state can be lost without consequences outweighing cost savings. Cold standby equipment is commonplace, typically in the form of computers of similar configuration at another location where the off-site backups are kept, tested, and restored in case of emergency. Increasingly, enterprises are recognizing the need for geographic diversity of personnel and systems and moving toward an approach where research and development systems feed change control systems that are identical to the systems in the field. The change control testing area can be turned into a live site as part of a recovery operation at any time, and since it is an exact copy it should work identically. When not used for restoration and recovery purposes, this site is used instead of sitting idle, so it is an even better value for the money than a standby site that is not used on a daily basis. Another alternative is a shared recovery site in which several companies share a computing facility used by any of them when their primary site is out of service. This is fine for extremely local disasters but becomes a contention issue in larger scale failures if not carefully planned.

2.6.3.2   Data in Motion

Data in motion may operate through physically secured wiring and infrastructure. If the physical security is adequate to the need, no additional measures are required. However, the vast majority of information in motion today travels over long distances through insecure infrastructure. In these cases additional protection is required as the consequences increase.

- **Extracting** the data from its at-rest state can be on a push or pull basis. Push systems, like email, have transmissions generated by the sender. In these systems, the sender is typically responsible for providing appropriate protection. Pull systems, like Web services, have user requests for transmission that are serviced by servers. These servers may take into account the user request and authorization based on identification and authentication to determine the proper protection associated with the transmission and then use protection as appropriate to the situation. However, most servers are not very good at it.
- **Encryption** is one of the main technologies used to protect information in transit. Because secure socket layer (SSL) encryption is so inexpensive and universally available, it has become a *de facto* standard for encryption of data in transmission. Encryption, if properly done (which it rarely is), allows communication to be kept confidential. But, on its own, it provides no protection other than confidentiality. Encryption gets its utility from a combination of the cryptographic algorithms used, the cryptographic protocols used to control the transmission sequences, and the implementation of those algorithms and protocols. While cryptographic algorithms are typically very hard to defeat if well chosen, cryptographic protocols often leave major vulnerabilities in systems, and implementations almost always fail to meet the need if attacked with a reasonable level of effort.
- **Authentication** is used to verify the validity of an assertion of identity. Surety varies with method and implementation. Authentication is usually done by verifying combinations of things that you are, have, and know or can do. Biometrics associate physical properties such as iris patterns, fingerprints, DNA structures, facial patterns, keystroke patterns, speech patterns, hand size and shape, footfalls, and other similar recognizable and differentiable characteristics of individuals. Most of these systems are useful for differentiating any of 1000 or so individuals from each other with reasonable numbers of false positives (acceptances) and false negatives (rejections), but they are poor at real-time identification of individuals. Therefore, their prime use in information protection is in verifying an identity and not in identifying an individual. Many biometrics can be easily spoofed, are not scalable, and use insecure infrastructure. Things that are

possessed typically include badges, software, digital certificates, time or use variant tokens, specialized hardware devices, cryptographic keys, and other physical keys or devices. They can all be stolen, and many of them can be duplicated or spoofed. Things that you know are limited because of human memory limitations which makes them potentially guessable. They typically have to be revealed in some form in order to be used, thus leading to their duplication and unauthorized use. Things that you can do are rarely used but can be effective. Multifactor authentication is used to increase the difficulty of attack at the cost of increased difficulty of use and reduced convenience. Such systems also have to have bypass capabilities for practical use in most enterprises. These bypass capabilities may be less well protected than the rest of the system, and they tend to aggregate risk, making the bypass mechanism a prime target for exploitation.

- **Transmission** of the data, possibly in cryptographic or other form, involves the translation of the data into a format and signal form suitable to the transport media. For example, for optical media bits have to be turned into modulations of optical signals. Transmission can be made over multiple channels and paths for diversity. In some cases spread spectrum techniques that change signal channels over time and introduce false signals into other channels to obfuscate messages are used to protect data from surveillance. Redundancy with spectrum spreading increases signal effectiveness over noisy channels and resists thin spectrum jamming, forcing jammers to increase their power over a wider spectrum to be effective and making them readily targetable as a result of their increased power footprint. Frequency and path hopping can be as effective as encryption at concealing content but they are less common than other techniques. Path diversity is harder to implement because of the increased cost associated with multiple paths and because the total number of paths available from any given physical location over wired infrastructure are limited to a very small number. Transmission often uses compression to increase effective bandwidth and may use cryptographic checksums on transmitted data to allow receivers to detect intermediate changes.

- **Transport** media has effects on accessibility. Radio is a broadcast medium allowing anyone within a signal-to-noise dictated distance to receive signals. In the case of satellite communication, this typically extends to at least one continent at a time, making the signal very widely available. For mechanisms like wireless WiFi and Bluetooth systems, the radius is on the order of a kilometer if the listener is skilled, and signal focusing (devices that focus signals directionally) or reduction (like special wall paint or building design) methods are not used. Wired media like cables or hubbed Ethernet systems are also broadcast media over the locations the wire extends to. Switched infrastructure uses point-to-switch signaling and switch-to-switch consolidation of signals, and allows SPAN ports to access all traffic, but under better control. Routed networks limit paths to relevant paths for the specific bit stream but can be redirected and used for broadcast and SPAN eavesdropping as well. Telephone transmission systems are line switched point-to-point communications with consolidation switch-to-switch, necessitating either central office or wire access for attack. Access is often available at the interface points and outside of structures.

Wires transmitting electromagnetic signals also generate induced signals that are readable without physical penetration of the cabling and even optical fibers can be read with laser interference methods, but fiber has far less cross-talk, requiring less separation of cabling for effective protection against high grade threats.

■ **Reception** of signals depends on environmental conditions that differ with the transport media. For many sort of optical, infrared, microwave, and similar radio techniques, atmospheric conditions have a substantial impact on reception. WiFi, Bluetooth, and mobile telephone technology have similar limitations. Signal strength for nonfixed systems varies substantially with location. Wired signals have reception problems under some environmental and atmospheric conditions, and power failures, and are subject to damage from Earth movement, electrical shock, and other similar causes.

■ **Verification** of transmitted information is typically done at a hardware level after translation into digital form through the use of checksums and cyclic redundancy check (CRC) codes. Under malicious attack, cryptographic checksums are necessary in order to verify that received data is identical to transmitted content, and these systems are subject to many of the same limitations as cryptographic systems. Verification of syntax, form, and values in context of the receiving system can also be used. Decompression is used to undo the compression associated with the transmission process. Unless verification is properly done, vulnerabilities in subsequent phases of transmission may be exploited.

■ **Decryption** is used to undo the encryption process that may be used prior to transmission so that received data is in usable form. Decryption keys must be protected in order to meaningfully decrypt content and prevent others from decrypting it.

■ **Delivery** of data to either storage or processing involves operating system operations that may include protection-related issues. Generally, access controls or similar protective measures are implemented in this process to assure that information is properly protected on delivery and stored with proper markings and protection settings to allow classification and access controls to operate properly.

2.6.3.3 Data in Use

Protection of data in use is problematic because it must be in a form that is useful for processing. There are some cases, like comparison to specific known values in password verification, where data can be left encrypted and have utility. But the vast majority of uses require that the data be readable. Data in use is rarely protected against modification beyond process separation mechanisms, because this is not supported by current processors.

■ **Validation** of data before use is critical to its proper use. Programs often make assumptions about inputs, and those assumptions are commonly exploited by attackers. Input should always be validated for syntax and value ranges based on program state. This is also used to detect inconsistencies and react to them.

- **Verification** is used to increase the surety level associated with data. It can take the form of redundant calculation, redundant data sourcing, or in some cases, a submit-commit cycle. Submit-commit cycles are typically used in conjunction with transaction systems. Submitted data is independently verified before a transaction is committed.
- **Transforms** on data are the dominant functions conjunction with the use of data. Inputs are mixed with state data to produce outputs and next states. The outputs represent transforms of the input sequence to an output sequence. Redundant processing is used in some cases to increase surety of results. In some cases processing uses checksums or state verification mechanisms to assure that transformations produce appropriate output. In use, data has to be protected from other data. This typically operates through operating system support of hardware mechanisms for process and memory separation.
- **Reconciliation** is used to verify the consistency of results. This is particularly important in financial transaction processing systems and other high-valued applications.
- **Instantiation** of data involves making copies of instances of data for different purposes. Multiple instances implies a need to mirror protective mechanisms and classifications across all instances.

2.6.4 Protection Process: Attack and Defense

Intentional attacks against information systems and technologies generally follow a pattern. The attacker seeks a target. Once a target is found, the attacker seeks vulnerabilities in the target and exploits them to gain privileges. These privileges are used either to exploit the access now available or to attempt to further expand access. Exploiting or expanding access can both be used to find additional targets and expand the scope of the attack, or they can be used more directly to induce consequences. There is another attack process that has been identified in which the attacker randomly tries an exploit against any target and proceeds based on the assumption that it worked. This attack process is very easy to detect and has a very low probability of success.

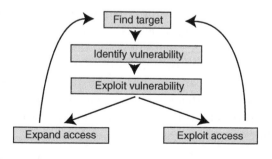

The attack process is carried out by threats using their capabilities and intents to attack system after system, ultimately leading to consequences. Defenses can sever the attack graph, or at least act to reduce the likelihood and increase the time associated with traversing the attack graph. The lighter areas in the depiction indicate defenses that cover (eliminate) threats, vulnerabilities, or consequences. In the example, even though there are vulnerabilities, threats, and consequences remaining uncovered, there is no path from threats through vulnerabilities to consequences. As a result, this protection will be effective even though it likely costs much less than eliminating all threats, vulnerabilities, and/or consequences (which is impossible).

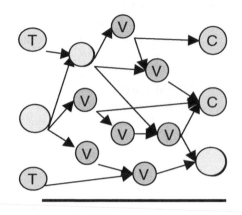

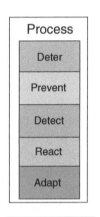

The defense process consists of deterrence, prevention, detection, reaction, and adaptation. Deterrence includes efforts to reduce the interest of attackers in specific targets. This involves psychological processes directed at the attacker and often uses deceptions of one sort or another. Prevention is typically attained by technical safeguards that limit access or function in some way. Detection should be designed to provide timely notice of event sequences that have potentially serious negative consequences. Reaction is the tactical response to attacks that are detected, which typically involves immediate actions to mitigate harm. Adaptation is a strategic response, typically involving architectural, process, or procedural changes.

2.6.4.1   Deter

Deterrence typically happens at the management level through decisions associated with public relations, business ventures, responses to other attacks, and corporate stances on issues that effect the decision process of the attacker. It includes preventing attacker awareness of targets, reducing interest in them as targets, and putting up barriers that make the attackers think targets are not worth the difficulty of attacking them, causing attackers to believe they will be caught and prosecuted if they try to attack, or to believe it is immoral or unethical to attack.

- **Perception** in the mind of threats is the target of any deterrence process. The goal is to influence attackers to prevent them from attacking. There are several common methods used to achieve this.

- **Deception** involves causing attackers to misperceive the object of their attacks. As a deterrent, deception can increase the workload and decrease the certainty of attack. Deception has proven effective in reducing the desire to attack, disrupting group processes among attack groups and increasing the cost to attackers.

- **The path of most resistance** deters most nondirected attackers who seek the path of least resistance. Even those who are determined tend to try simpler things first and move on when the going gets tough. Only skilled, directed professionals attack hard targets with determination.

- **Arrest** of perpetrators and widespread publication of arrests are the most effective deterrents against the estimated one third of people who will break the rules if they think there is little likelihood of punishment.

- **Prosecution** increases the perception that attack will be harshly met. Unfortunately, too many executives who get involved in abuse of systems end up unpunished even though those who work for them are more likely to get prosecuted. Prosecution of executives and the threat of criminal prosecution under Sarbanes-Oxley have provided a dramatic change in deterrence of corporate crimes and have dramatically increased the adoption of regulatory mandated protective measures.

- **Sanctions** should be provided for by policy. They should be clear and uniform, and identify those sanctions with specific acts so as to deter those acts. Policy should also require that these sanctions be read, understood, and agreed to by those who agree to work for the enterprise so that it becomes a term of employment and is included in contracts.

- **Awareness of sanction policies and consequences** of actions are effective and should be included in awareness programs to help deter criminal acts by employees and other authorized workers.

2.6.4.2   Prevent

Prevention of attacks is done by stopping the attacker from finding a target, identifying and exploiting vulnerabilities, and expanding or exploiting privilege. Techniques used to prevent attacks are identified in the security database at http://all.net/. These techniques can be used to sever attack graphs.

- **Deception** techniques prevent attackers from finding targets, identifying vulnerabilities, and expanding or exploiting privileges. They are predominantly used today in preventing target detection by making it harder for an attacker to differentiate a legitimate target from a false target. Once an attacker is detected attacking a false target, real targets are made unavailable to the attacker, thus forming a detection/response loop that acts to prevent further attack attempts from finding any real targets. Against random attacks, deception can be used to cause any random attack to have a low probability of success, followed by acting to cut off further attack graphs.

- **Firewalls** are designed to cut off attack graphs that start on one side of the firewall and go to another side of it. They act as prevention mechanisms at the perimeters of enclaves. In different terms, the firewall defines the perimeter of an enclave. They prevent the identification of targets and exploitation of target vulnerabilities by preventing information flow between the attacker on one side of the firewall and their target on another side of the firewall. They limit the expansion and exploitation of network access by limiting the range of other network locations that can be reached and the manner in which they can be reached.

■ **Authentication** is used to prevent an attacker from doing what an authorized user can do. More and more sure authentication techniques are used to increase the level of certainty that the user is who they claim to be. This extends to software acting on behalf of users as well as in roles that are only associated with automated systems.

■ **Authorization** associates authorities with authenticated identities. Authorization mechanisms include both the technical mechanisms that allow an identified and authenticated user to perform functions with data and the mechanisms used to grant, revoke, and alter those authorities. The administrative control over authorities is often the weak link in a system of controls. Authorizations are often set incorrectly and fail to properly associate the clearances of the user, the certainty of the authentication of that user, and the classification of the data. As a result, users have too little authority to get their job done or more authority than they require for the tasks they need to perform. The principle of least privilege asserts that the latter is inappropriate, and the former implies a lack of proper business function. But getting precision in authorization is difficult because of the complexity of systems and the mismatch between technical protections and management intent. A typical system has millions of protection bits and inadequate technical tools to manage them. And those protection bits usually control technical mechanisms that are too large grained and incommensurate with policies. Finer granularity is achievable at the cost of more time and space. Commensurability is not obtainable because computers do not have mechanisms to operate on intent. Arbitrary rules can be reasonable for people making decisions (i.e., in an emergency where granting this person access to that data might save many lives, grant the access) but trying to codify that in terms of things that computers process is infeasible for the foreseeable future.

■ **Access control** mechanisms are typically based on a subject/object model. Subjects are typically user identities associated with processes. Objects are usually devices, files, records, or fields. The access control might be based on any number of implementations, ranging from capabilities lists to access control lists to group and user identities associated with processes and files, but they can all be modeled as subject/object matrices in which each subject is granted a set of rights with respect to each object. This is a stateless model in which the sequence of events that got the subject to where they are has no effect on the rights they have with respect to objects. Models with state dependencies are far more complex and have not been implemented to date.

■ **Use controls**, in the sense of technical prevention mechanisms, are programmed mechanisms that associate functions with situations. For example, when a Web server intermediates between a browser and a database, the Web server is often granted access adequate to perform any of the functions it can perform for any use it is designed to facilitate. This lack of access control is (usually poorly) compensated for by the Web server using applications that only use appropriate functions for the situation. These controls tend to be far weaker than operating system controls because they depend on situation dependent code that is less tested, in larger quantity, less controlled in its development, and more easily exploited than typical access control mechanisms. However, these use controls can make more situation-dependent decisions.

- High-speed **intrusion prevention systems** (IPSs) are really just systems that detect intrusions and respond to them before they are exploitable. IPS depends on adequate and appropriate detection of intrusions, an OODA loop that is fast enough to respond before serious negative consequences arise, and a response that is not exploitable to the advantage of the attacker and that is effective at preventing the serious negative consequences. Today, there are systems that can detect certain classes of known intrusions and react in time to sever the attack graphs associated with them; however, they produce false positives, false negatives, and can be exploited for reflexive control, typically resulting in denial of services to legitimate uses.

- Architecture acts as a preventive measure if properly implemented. **Separation** as an architectural principle is one of the keys to success. For example, by separating networks into areas based on the need to communicate, attacks that otherwise deny services on a large scale are contained to the areas in which they first appear. This limits damage and provides time and controls to help mitigate the problem. The separation of audit from control from data is also central to proper network operations and to meeting regulatory compliance requirements. Separation tends to be far less expensive to implement and operate than more active alternatives, it is more certain to work, and it tends to solve problems over longer periods of time, reducing churn associated with many other more active controls.

- **Surety** is a measurable basis for asserting the certainty with which the protective measure will successfully perform the function it is intended to perform and no other. Higher surety indicates more certainty. Different protective measures have different surety levels and costs. Generally, defenders should favor higher surety at lower cost, like choosing separation mechanisms in architecture over IPS approaches when they cover the same attack graphs. But very often there are trade offs between cost and surety, and in these cases the decision is not so clear.

2.6.4.3   Detect

The fundamental purpose of detection is to identify event sequences with potentially serious negative consequences in time to mitigate those consequences to within acceptable levels. Unfortunately, this is not how most current detection systems work. Rather, they detect what they are able to detect regardless of the utility of those detections.

Detection is an enormously problematic area. Ideally, detection would never be used because prevention would be perfect. However, we do not live in an ideal world As a result, detection is necessary, at a minimum, to provide redundancy for preventive techniques so that when they fail there is a chance the failure can be detected and mitigated. But detection technologies have increasingly become preferred over prevention technologies by many decision makers for a variety of good and not-so-good reasons.

Fundamental issues associated with detection make it problematic. For any of the more interesting things that current detection systems try to detect (e.g., viruses, spam, intrusions, anomalies, spyware, etc.) there are a potentially infinite number of false positives (false alarms) and false negatives (missed alarms) for any finite detection time. This means that detection always has to deal with these issues in order to be effective and that response has to take this possibility into account.

Detection of attacks of this sort is, and will always be, unreliable; it takes time, causes delays, and is costly to operate. Detection of attacks generally has to be updated because attackers adapt to detection mechanisms. This means that they must be actively attended to in order to remain effective. Detection implies response and response implies investigation, so the indirect costs of detection are high when many detections take place. Ideally, detection operates in a relatively quiet environment with little noise and few attacks to detect. But when used as a substitute for an effective prevention mechanism, detection is very expensive to operate, uncertain, and complex to get right.

There is, however, a chicken-or-egg problem associated with detection. Without detection, many attacks go unnoticed in the tactical time frame and may never be associated with their consequences. For example, an attack that reveals pricing information and causes no other harm will be reflected in a more competitive sales environment, It may seem like the competition is heating up, and eventually you may even go out of business, which has happened from this very cause. The problem is that without detection, justifying costs of prevention is difficult, and effective prevention means that little will be detected, and most of it will be unimportant. So in order to justify more budget for protection, more detection is used, the numbers of apparent attack attempts increase, and the case for more defenses grows. As a manager, the hard thing to do is to be effective at preventing and detecting attacks with potentially serious negative consequences while getting adequate funding to meet the need without resorting to scare tactics or creating false impressions in order to get proper budget.

- **Host-based detection** resides at endpoints. It has the advantage of having host state information available for its analysis, but there is the disadvantage of not having access to related information from other hosts. Thus, it lacks the context to understand the larger picture. Hosts tend to have excess performance available, and thus host-based detection can use more computer time per host. In the aggregate, far more unused computer time is available in hosts than in most other places. Host-based detection can look at stored state information over long time frames, giving it more potential for deeper inspection.

- **Network-based detection** operates based on network traffic. It has the advantage of being able to cover many hosts with one mechanism in one location but the disadvantage of not having host state information available for situation analysis. The performance of a network-based detection system is limited because the bandwidth must be significant in order to gain the advantages of centralized detection. The ability to retain historical information, relate information over long time frames, and correlate information from many different hosts is limited by memory and performance, which means that as bandwidth goes up, the analytical capacity per packet goes down. The leverage gained by centralizing the function is paid for by a reduction in available analytical power.

- **Intrusion detection** is a term associated with known techniques that can be codified in specific terms but, of course, many sorts of intrusions only become known to defenders after they are detected by other means, and many are never known. In terms of detection, current systems typically only detect known intrusions and, specifically, detect only a very small class of intrusion types that are detectable by observing specific event sequences of short length from the same user. While research has produced far more advanced intrusion detection techniques, they have not been substantially implemented in commercial products. Most known intrusion detection techniques are easily bypassed. For example, in an article written several years ago, 50 ways to defeat intrusion detection systems were identified, almost all of which work against almost all current detection systems. See "The 50 Ways Series" at http://all.net/ for details.

- **Anomaly detection** seeks to detect events and sequences of events that are different by some measure of significance from "normal" events and event sequences. In law enforcement there is a saying "JDLR" which stands for "just doesn't look right." When something just doesn't look right, investigation is necessary in order to figure out what's going on. The same is true in detection for information protection. Anomaly detection leads to investigation. The false-positive and false-negative problem is reflected in a quantity of detections over time. Too many detections overruns the available investigative response capacity of the defenders, while too few detections reduces the justification for that capacity. Thus the detection thresholds are often set to match the investigative capacity of the organization rather than to reflect the value of the detections. A proper feedback system should use the results of investigations to determine what thresholds on which sorts of anomalies justify alarms, and the system and staff should be adapted to those needs rather than using staff levels as a basis for choosing what events and event sequences to alarm on. Automated response based on anomaly detection is also problematic. Without investigation, anomalies are not to be trusted as a basis for action other than investigation. In situations where anomalies are very serious and known to cause serious negative consequences in time frames that are short, automated response must be carefully predetermined to assure that it will always result in a fail safe condition.

- **Behavior** produces externally observable events. These are the events that detection systems try to observe. Limits on observation are associated with the limits of sensors, the limits of translation of sensor data into representations, and the limits of detection system capabilities for analysis of sensor data. Behaviors associated with systems and people in situations are typically predictable to within some limits, and this predictability leads to detection of deviations.

- **Situation** provides context that is used to determine the acceptability and normalcy of behaviors. There are sets of situations in which certain behaviors are acceptable, but codifying all of the situations associated with each behavior at fine granularity is unfeasible. As a result, situations are generally split into large-grained classes of situations.

- **Patterns** are matched with event sequences in context to determine if the events are to trigger a detection.

- **Heuristics** are sequential machines used as a more general form of pattern matching mechanism. They are typically coded as sequences of triggering conditions and actions, but may be arbitrary state machines.

- **History** is often used to calibrate anomaly detection systems, and historical data is sometimes recorded and replayed for calibration purposes.

- **Authority** of users to perform tasks is sometimes used to differentiate between legitimate and illegitimate uses. By using detection to identify cases when authority is apparently exceeded or does not match actions, attacks that bypass protections can often be detected.

- **Identity** is sometimes mapped into event sequences so that the identity of an individual can be used to differentiate legitimate from illegitimate event sequences.

- **Collection** of data for detection and collection of forensic data related to the detection process is necessary in order to perform analysis and to assure that adequate record-keeping is done for legal and regulatory purposes.

- **Preservation** of data is typically required for its use in any subsequent legal action. This should be done as part of normal business record recording processes and should be well structured and documented to assure that it is not easily challenged in court.

- **Fusing** data together is required for detection of all but the simplest of known attack patterns. This typically starts with session-level fusion so that parts of the same session are translated into input and output sequences as associated with each finite state machine (hardware device, protocol element, software program, or application) for analysis of its impact on that machine. At the next level of abstraction, changes in these machines should be fused against other changes in the total environment to identify implications of those changes relative to expectations. This level of fusion is almost never used in current systems; however, experimental systems at this level have been implemented.

- **Analysis** processes are used to match fused data against criteria to determine what constitutes a detection and what properties to associate with those detections. Analysis for a wide range of classes of attacks have been determined to be undecidable so there are and will always be infinite numbers of false positives and negatives for general purpose computing environments. However, most high valued systems in use in enterprises are really not used for unlimited purposes and adequate characterization of their operation can be used to dramatically reduce false positives and negatives. Whereas the integrity of data is a function of intent, in many systems intent can be well and clearly defined for all but the most unusual situations.

■ **Attribution** of actions to actors is critical for the association of detections to those responsible and for the process that follows.

2.6.4.4 React

Reaction is dependent on detection. Without some sort of detection, there is nothing to react to, and if detection is not accurate or timely, the reaction will also have problems with being appropriate and timely. Particular problems arise with automated response systems because they form reflexes of the enterprise information infrastructure. If these reflexes can be triggered by attackers they can be used to induce undesired responses that damage the enterprise. A classic, and one of the most easily exploited examples, is the introduction of false packets into a network so as to cause the detection system to asses that an attack is underway by one critical system against another critical system it is linked to. The detection system identifies the packets as an attack. This, in turn, induces an automatic response of cutting off the attacking system from the victim of its attacks. The result is the severing of communications between two critical interdependent systems. This problem stems from a combination of factors, often including poor design, inaccurate detection and attribution, the need to react quickly and automatically to certain classes of attack in order to limit damage, and a lack of proper architectural planning and response analysis.

■ **Investigation** of detected event sequences is necessary in order to determine an appropriate reaction. For certain classes of sequences, automated responses are developed, but this allows reflexive control attacks. Unfortunately, these same sequences in different contexts may require immediate response in order to limit harm, so investigative processes have to be balanced with immediacy. Investigative processes also have a tendency to produce far more information than a simple explanation of the event sequence of interest. In case after case, seemingly trivial detections have led to investigations that became larger and larger scope. In many cases, these became large-scale criminal or civil prosecutions. Investigations typically start with a triage effort by internal incident response team members and follow through until there is reason to believe that something involving inappropriate behavior has taken place. At that point the investigation has to be handed over to investigative professionals in order to result in a positive outcome. Many amateur investigations end up producing serious problems. These include legal liabilities, harassment suits, inadequate evidence, loss of critical forensic data, and inability to prosecute. When insiders are involved in cases requiring investigations, the potential for investigative leaks and cover-ups increases dramatically. Unless there are professional internal investigators on staff, outside private investigative teams that specialize in computer-related investigations are usually used.

Investigations are usually carried out by, through, or in conjunction with corporate legal counsel.

■ **Assessments** are undertaken in response to high-consequence detected incidents at two levels. An initial assessment and any number of small follow-on assessments are often undertaken as part of triage efforts to determine who to contact, how far to escalate responses, who to get involved, and so forth. In addition, incidents sometimes generate an awareness that results in more strategic assessments such as IPPAs. Although this is not the optimal approach to resolving enterprise issues, many CISOs and others use the response process to justify such assessments because these are the only times that management shows a willingness to spend enough money on such an issue to get it done.

■ **Refocus** of attention and resources often occur in response. The details of each event in context drive processes in different directions, cause sensors to be adapted, thresholds to be changed, forensic data to be generated and analyzed, and so forth.

■ **Coordination** is required for many complex investigations as they may spread to involve large numbers of systems, some not even under the control of the enterprise. Coordination of response processes for timing of technical steps is required. Responses may have to be coordinated across the enterprise at a management level. Legal coordination is required at any point where humans get involved or when it is determined that the event sequence is not just a technical flaw of some sort. Investigative coordination is required with law enforcement and the legal system in many cases. Physical security and HR coordination get involved when employees or contractors are involved. Line management gets involved and must coordinate administrative actions. Executives get involved when consequences are high enough.

■ **Opinions** are generated during response processes, and these opinions are used to make decisions about how to proceed with the process.

■ **Advice** is often given to managers and executives at all levels in order to help them make decisions about actions to be taken, both in tactical incident response and as a result of investigative processes.

■ **Reporting** and presentation of detected information and related materials is critical to the response process. Data presentation plays a particularly important part of the reporting associated with response. When a user reports a problem, this is a response to a sequence of events. User reporting is responsible for a significant portion of all detected incidents today. Tracking of reported incidents is used to detect coordinated attacks, and incident reporting data is often used to justify further efforts in information protection. For some events, like the discovery of contraband or the possession of material that is illegal to possess, immediate reporting to legal authorities may be required as well. Legal counsel should be involved in this process.

■ **Covering of vulnerabilities** is commonly used in incident response. A typical example is the creation of a firewall rule to limit the use of a port associated with an attack while repairs are done to mitigate the attack.

■ **Disabling of features**, capabilities, or select systems is sometimes used to mitigate the short-term effects of an attack. This is typically used when the value of the service is outweighed by the damage of the attack. It is also used during some repair processes to prevent further exploitation until the repair is completed.

- **Push back** is used to try to force the action closer to the attacker. Typically, an attack is detected near its target, and as the path toward the target is identified, protective measures are moved closer and closer to the attacker until the attacker is cut off, rather than the target's being cut off. This strategy reduces wasted bandwidth at the target and in intervening infrastructure, but it is problematic against most distributed coordinated attacks in use today. They are so distributed that cutting them off beyond border routers disrupts normal operations.

- **Deception** is a viable response strategy against many attackers, and those who have used deception under the title of "honeypots" or similar appealing names have been successful at convincing management of its utility and appeal. Deception done properly can be used in a tactical as well as strategic manner and can lead attackers far astray. Depending on situational specifics, deception can be a very useful counterintelligence tool; however, the cost goes up as the fidelity of the deception increases, and substantial expertise is required in order to be effective against high quality attackers with deception.

- **Mitigation** is typically associated with repairs of weaknesses in systems that allow them to be attacked. Of course, all of the responses described here are part of the overall mitigation effort, but repairs are notionally the path taken to mitigate most harm as a semipermanent fix. Mitigation of faults in an operational system is several orders of magnitude more expensive than proper design. The deeper problem is that many attacks do not involve weaknesses, but rather exploit the normal operations. Unless systems are designed so as to avoid unlimited flexibility and control changes, many sorts of attacks will continue to be mitigated on a one-by-one basis.

- **Administrative changes** to systems are also typical of response processes. Usually, this involves cleaning up many side effects of the attack, often in a highly manual and time consuming process.

- **Prosecution** of attackers is last step in response and typically takes years, if it is pursued at all. It is rarely pursued because the benefit to the enterprise is only indirect, and the cost in time and inconvenience is substantial. When prosecution is avoided, the result is a criminal that continues to commit crimes.

2.6.4.5 Adapt

Adaptations typically happen at an architectural level and operate as a long-term strategic response to enterprise needs. Whereas rapid adaptations are used in some cases, these usually result in poor solutions that are ineffective and expensive even though they may fulfill an administrative need.

- **Management** of overall information architecture is critical to any adaptation. A management and technical team typically oversee architecture and zoning to make strategic adaptations. This team is often augmented by specialized security architects.

■ **Process** requirements for any architectural change require approvals of all sorts, from zoning board functions to design approvals and so on. An excellent source for design process criteria is the NSTISSI series of standards on security design processes for classified systems. Whereas most enterprise systems don't have a need to meet this level of rigor, reduction in rigor is easier than trying to develop a new process from scratch. NSTISSI standards include four different sorts of individuals with different responsibilities:

Designated approving authorities describe the purpose, applicability, responsibilities, and minimum performance standards for approving authorities. They cover legal liabilities, policies, threats, incidents, access, administrative responsibility, communications security, tempest protection, life cycle management, continuity of operations, and risk management.

Systems administrators cover purpose, applicability, responsibilities, and minimum standards for administrators. These include access controls, administrative requirements, audits, operations, contingencies, and platform-specific security features and procedures.

Information system security officers cover purpose, scope, applicability, responsibilities, and performance standards. They include (1) maintaining a plan for site security improvements and progress toward meeting the accreditation, (2) ensuring that systems are operated, used, maintained, and disposed of in accordance with security policies and practices, (3) ensuring that the system is accredited and certified if it processes sensitive information, (4) ensuring that users and system support personnel have the required security clearances, authorization, and need-to-know, are indoctrinated, and are familiar with internal security practices before access is granted, (5) enforcing security policies and safeguards on all personnel having access, (6) ensuring audit trails are reviewed periodically (e.g., weekly, daily), and audit records are archived for future reference, (7) if required, initiating protective or corrective measures, reporting security incidents in accordance with policy, (8) reporting the security status of the system, and (9) evaluating known vulnerabilities to ascertain if additional safeguards are needed.

System Certifiers responsibilities cover purpose, applicability, responsibilities, and minimum performance standards. These include documenting mission needs, registering the new application for tracking purposes, negotiation of security requirements, preparing a plan for accreditation, supporting system development, performing certification analysis, recommending certification, evaluating compliance, and maintaining the certification over time.

■ **Engineering** approaches to architecture adaptation include the need for compatibility with legacy systems, meeting cost constraints, integration with enterprise operational capabilities and systems, and understanding how to analyze architectural measures against protection needs. The CMM-SEC approach is also a design and engineering methodology that can be applied to track and measure adaptation.

- **Architecture** of the enterprise network and the application under adaptation require a detailed understanding of existing enterprise information technology architecture, a clear understanding of protection requirements that are driving adaptation, and the history that led to the situation on the ground. Security expertise relevant to the architectural issues is a must, but in many cases, architectures go from bad to worse when security engineers ignore the context of the systems. The goal of adaptation should be to provide a reasonably smooth and low cost transition from one architectural state to the next. The overall path may take a long time to follow. Along the way, it is critical to take steps that move toward the objective without disrupting the organization beyond its ability to adapt to the changes.
- **Organizational adaptation** is sometimes called for as a part of adaptation. Many failures in protection are the result of inadequate separation of duties or similar failures to follow basic principles. These are often driven by organizational issues such as power struggles between managers and executives. When organizations have to be adapted, skill at exercising influence comes to the fore.

2.6.4.6 Detect/React Loop

The detect/react loop is particularly critical to the effectiveness of the response process because if it is fast enough it provides prevention, if it is too slow it is ineffective, and if the attacker can tune the attack to it, it can create positive feedback to amplify the attack.

- **OODA loops**, otherwise known as the Boyd cycle, dominate much of the discussion surrounding this issue because they are a convenient, if imprecise, way to discuss the issue in understandable terms. Observation, orientation, decision, and action (OODA) express the process by which events outside a system interact with a system. But, of course, there are many systems involved in typical attack and defense processes, so there are many OODA loops underway at any given time. Systems exist in layers of context, and response processes happen at all layers. Attackers and defenders have limits associated with times between different events. Performance limitations of computing systems and algorithms play into the issue. Human performance is also an issue in many situations.
- **Autonomics** are used in cases when human reaction time is too slow for effective reaction, and the situation can be accurately characterized enough to allow for effective and nonharmful response that fails in a safe mode. An example of autonomic systems used in a high risk situation is the computers that control the space shuttle during its hypersonic S-curves as it enters the atmosphere. Because reaction times have to be so fast (milliseconds) that humans cannot maintain control on their own, the dynamically unstable system has to be managed by computers. But computers fail, and a single computer failure in this critical operation could cause the shuttle to disintegrate. So redundant computers that detect other computer failures and react to them very quickly are used. Unfortunately,

most enterprises do not think though their autonomic responses this well, but fortunately, there tend to be clearer fail safe conditions for most enterprises, and few of their systems cause such large negative consequences so quickly.

- **Operations** have slower Boyd cycles in response to event sequences than autonomics, but many operational mistakes have led to dire consequences. For example, operational errors have brought down large computer networks for hours to days. The brittleness of operational decisions with respect to information infrastructure implies the desire for a way to check things out before instantiating changes. Thus, change control is commonly used in operational responses to assure that changes can be undone and that changes don't cause more harm than good. Ultimately, simulation systems would be most helpful in this arena, and some networks have such systems in place for verifying changes before testing and doing larger numbers of simulations than would be possible to cover by testing alone. Most large enterprises that handle high valued information in automatic systems for a long time have solid testbeds for testing operational changes and have strong change control to assure that this testing is completed before changes are made to the operational network. However, in emergencies, certain classes of changes are sometimes made anyway, and some of these emergency changes cause more harm than the problem they were intended to solve. Risk management is necessary as part of the decision to forgo change management.

- **Organizations** have far longer OODA loops. The need for committee decisions, meetings, verification with legal processes and policies, and the rest of the organizational process that supports information protection, requires patience that is sometimes quite taxing. In many cases, the detect react cycle for organizations is so broken that individuals responsible for criminal acts continue those acts and are given time to get away. In some cases, they are even notified of the pending actions by the process or team members with mixed loyalties. In these cases speeding up the process may not be feasible, and slow processes lead to extended problem periods. While it is advisable to act quickly in information protection responses at an organizational level, this is only really feasible in hierarchies when the top decision-maker makes a rapid decision. This also tends to have high risks for all involved, tends to reduce the amount of legitimate consideration required for high-valued decisions, and creates more tension than is generally desired in a large organization.

2.6.5 Protection Process: Work Flows

Protection process is typically implemented in terms of a set of work flows; standardized event sequences with inputs, state, outputs, and systems that take state and input to produce output and next state — with the explicit purpose of carrying out the processes identified for protection. There are many work flow systems available, and they typically handle help desk operations or other ticketing systems; similar mechanisms have been around for many years in the legal profession, medicine, aerospace, and other fields.

Manual work flow systems were commonplace until the last several years. Many persist and will for a long time to come.

The advantages of automated work flow systems for security come in several forms. They assure that work gets done in the proper sequence, they can act to assure that approvals are properly undertaken prior to actions, they can provide automated provisioning integration for automatable work flows like adding user identities based on roles and similar functions, they can document the entire process, allow verification, help to reduce the work load for audit, and provide support for process improvement. However, because of their central role in operational aspects of protection, they also form risk aggregation points that pose significant risk. For example, identity management solutions that automate some limited components of security work flow associated with access controls can be attacked to cause all access to cease, to grant access to unauthorized individuals, to destroy the information functions of an organization, or to disrupt operations in automated manufacturing or processing facilities. Providing adequate surety for these systems and disaggregating risks by creating sets of these systems with zones of control and potentially overlapping authorities is complex and problematic but necessary for the enterprise that wishes to succeed in light of the realities of threats in the information world.

2.6.5.1   Work to Be Done

Many facets of information protection exist, and the work that has to be done for all of these facets comprises a very significant portion of the total effort in information protection. Work has to be described and standardized in order to fit into work flow systems, and this itself is a very substantial effort. There are some partial work flow systems that exist for security, but they are nowhere near the level of completeness required for an enterprise. They cover only a small subset of the overall work flow of the enterprise security operation. This guidebook includes high-level overviews of hundreds of processes that all have to be codified into work flows in order for them to be properly handled in a systematic manner for an enterprise. For the small- or medium-sized business this guidebook can be combined with our security metrics book to form a set of checklists for many of the common functions; they have been used for that purpose by some early adopters.

2.6.5.2   Process for Completion and Options

For each item of work to be done, a process for completion should be defined including the conditions for its invocation; times associated with different actions to be undertaken; primary and auxiliary contacts for performing the identified tasks; optional processes for emergency, standard, and exceptional conditions including appeals processes and overrides; and enough details to allow any authorized and properly trained or competent person to carry out the work. The processes should identify points for workers to certify that work has been done and for those who verify work that is to be certified to do so and notify the system of the verification.

2.6.5.3   Control Points and Approval Requirements

Most processes have control points of one sort or another. For example, a worker may prepare all of the elements for a building to be wired for electrical systems but until the building inspector comes and approves of the plan and of the building ready to be wired, the wiring waits. In information protection there are similar control points defined, typically when risks beyond thresholds of the level of the current worker are reached. The approval process should then identify someone with adequate authority and knowledge to make a reasonable and prudent decision about the risk, identify the risk and the options to the authorized person or people, and seek their approval or rejection or optional paths. In some cases multiple approvals or more complex voting systems may be used, and timeliness issues may require actions be taken urgently. Presumably, the overall system has to be able to handle this in order to be effective in these cases.

2.6.5.4   Appeals Processes and Escalations

Work flows have to have suitable provisions for appeals and escalations when something that one person wants to have done is at odds with someone in the approval path. Although most processes don't get appealed in hierarchical systems because of the nature of the structure, in matrix organizations there may be many paths to getting work done, and in networked organizations the organic nature of the process often allows many paths to getting something done. But even in a hierarchical process there will be times when escalation is used; for example, when timeliness is an issue and normal approval paths are not available in a timely enough fashion.

2.6.5.5   Authentication Requirements and Mechanisms

The quality and quantity of authentication associated with different functions typically varies across a wide spectrum. For example, a simple lookup of the work to be done might require only a user identity and password, whereas the ability to change a work order may require an additional authentication such as the presentation of a time variant password from a secure token. For some actions, physical presence may be required and this may mandate a third party authentication to certify presence along with biometric data and other similar methods. The work flow system has to allow the use of different authentication mechanisms to support the different levels of surety required to perform different operations.

2.6.5.6   Authorization and Context Limitations

Authorizations associated with identified subjects under different levels of authentication may change with context (see details of context elsewhere) and different situations within work flows. The work flow system has to be capable of handling complexities associated with the specific identified needs of data owners for access to the resources necessary to do work, and in some cases, alternative sources with different authentication requirements may be sought because of circumstance. For example, if time is of import and any two of eight approvers are adequate to the need for a process to continue, the work flow might request responses from all eight authorizers. The authorizers can be notified that the work has been approved once two have approved, so that they don't have to look at the issue if it is already settled. Similarly, context may change during the process, thus changing the approval requirements and appropriate methods must be used to properly deal with these situations. The work flow system should also help to prioritize work so that more important or time-critical work is given proper priority.

2.6.5.7   Work Flow Documentation and Audit

The work flow system should provide documentation of what was done and what is to be done, and allow this information to be read for audit purposes as appropriate. Detailing should be available to the specific actions taken by specific individuals at specific times, the approvals required and obtained, and the work flow requirements of the situation at the time should be documented so that all of the information needed to validate an action after the fact can be made available to the reviewer or auditor. Thus, everything needed to determine what was done, why, when, how, where, and under what situational circumstances should be available to check on any specific process undertaken or all of the processes of the system.

2.6.5.8   Control and Validation of the Engine(s)

Whether work-flow mechanisms are manual or automated, the mechanisms that control the processes have to be controlled, verified, validated, tested, reviewed, and tracked to assure that they do what they are supposed to do. This includes both the normal operation of these mechanisms and all of the exception conditions and malicious sequences that might circumvent the system at every level of its operation. For example, if work flows are implemented using a paper system to cover regular backups of systems, the process will typically involve the use of a piece of paper that indicates what to do on a given shift. The shift workers then use the checklist, perhaps doing a backup and reflecting that on the checklist with date, time, tape number, and initials. The verification may be done by going to the proper tape number and restoring its contents to a test system to verify that it has the data it should have from that time and date, and that it properly restores. Verification of this activity by random sample will validate that the mechanism is being used and operating properly. Additional malicious abuse testing might include seeing whether making a false entry causes a backup to not be done (for example, a worker could claim to have done the work on a prior shift even though he did not do it and cause backups to go undone) or by taking away the sheets of paper and determining whether a work around is used to still do the backups and how the escalation process works in that circumstance.

2.6.5.9   Risk Aggregation in the Engine(s)

Automated work flow systems tend to aggregate risk by centralizing and unifying the processes that the system supports, by combining the information and capabilities of the work flows into a single computer or at a single location, by unifying the administrative aspects of managing those systems, by using common operating environments with common mode failure mechanisms, by combining previously separate mechanisms, and by creating dependencies on the work flow system for proper execution of work. At the same time, these systems reduce costs, increase efficiency, improve auditability and account-ability, reduce time to get many tasks done by using computer communications to replace paper processes, provide for more efficient and effective backups of the work flows, and so forth. The question for executive management and risk management to answer is how much risk can be aggregated before additional protective measures are required. As a rule of thumb, and based on the notion that the surety should match the risk, as risk gets to the medium level, medium surety techniques should be used. As the work flow system reaches to risk levels where single individuals can no longer be permitted to make decisions, those systems need to be made multiperson control, the risk disaggregated by using multiple work flow systems, or other compensating controls must be used.

2.6.6 Protective Mechanisms

Protective mechanisms are the technical mechanisms that are directly in contact with or in control of the content, threats, vulnerabilities, or consequences, and assure the security of the content and its utility while supporting its business utility with minimal friction.

2.6.6.1   Perception

Perception-related defenses are typically used to influence the attacker and as such they are directed at the attacker. Although outsiders are subject to many defenses, even insiders can be affected by perception. Perception is a rather substantial field and much research has been done in this area; however, the basics from an information protection standpoint can be characterized in terms of:

- **Obscurity**: By making facilities, people, systems, and other elements of the information infrastructure and capabilities of the enterprise difficult to understand and find, it becomes harder for the attackers to locate and attack or exploit them. Although obscurity as a defense is often viewed negatively by some members of the information protection community, obscurity plays a critical role in almost all protection schemes. If everything is known about a system and its defenses it is indeed far easier to defeat than if it is less well known to the attacker.

- **Profile**: Keeping a low profile is very helpful in defeating many attackers. While many business leaders and experts make their living largely by being public personalities, for most people, keeping a low profile is relatively easy to do. Buildings that have data centers, for example, should not be marked as such, because by marking the building or making its purpose easy to understand, attackers are given an easy method for target identification. In addition, random attacks and attacks by many group threats tend to be oriented toward high profile targets, and those attackers can be avoided by this approach. Even against insiders, computer centers with large glass walls in imposing spaces may end up being targets of opportunity or foci of resentment. Keeping locations with high value obscure can be highly effective at reducing insider threats to physical infrastructure just as keeping the names and locations of financial and critical systems obscure can reduce the number of insiders likely to try to attack them.

- **Appearance**: Many people have misimpressions of enterprises that stem from historical information, rumors, competitive advertisements, industry norms, or small numbers of negative contacts. These people may become threats if they believe that the enterprise has done something wrong or illegal. The appearance of an enterprise, a system, a facility, or a business venture has a direct effect on the set of threats that are likely to be faced by it. Although there will always be some threats that will get past appearances, many will not.

- **Deception**: The general field of deception for information protection is substantial and growing. It is based on the notion that there are error mechanisms in automated systems and people that can be exploited to induce faults in their processes. These error mechanisms can be effectively exploited to defend systems from attack. A common deception is the use of a firewall to suppress the information about internal systems, and another one is using the same reply for a failed password as a failed user identification in a login. Deceptions can also be use to induce false signals, for example, to disrupt threat-induced network intelligence efforts or to present easily exploited systems so that attackers will exploit them instead of higher valued systems.

2.6.6.2   Structure

The structure of networks, systems, applications, facilities, and businesses can effectively limit risks. These structural mechanisms are used to create structures that provide some number of layers of defense against attacks from different sources. Of course a fundamental thing to understand about structures is that those inside any given area of a structure are essentially past the barriers, and those barriers are of no effect except in their role as separators. Thus, the separation mechanisms lead to zones that are differentiated from each other by those barrier mechanisms and form a set of logical spaces.

- **Mandatory or discretionary access controls** are mechanisms that enforce separation controls based on subject/object models that limit access of subjects to objects. Discretionary controls are controlled by the user while mandatory ones are controlled by the system itself. Mandatory controls generally follow a control scheme like the Bell Lapadula model used in the Trusted System Evaluation Criteria that is designed to protect users from getting access to higher classification levels than their clearances allow. Discretionary access controls like those in Unix and similar systems allow users to set protections of files to determine whether they are private to the user, the user's group, or not private.

- **Information flow limitations** are used to form barriers between regions as opposed to the lower-level subject/object controls of typical access control mechanisms. This is usually used for network separation, as in the use of virtual local area network (VLAN) technologies with rate shaping to separate areas of networks, or the use of router-based controls to limit network addresses, physical interfaces, and network ports across routers or switches. Rate limits on networks are used to limit denial of services attacks, and routing can be used to force specific traffic to travel along specific routes.

- **Digital diodes and similar mechanisms** provide high assurance that information can only go where it is supposed to go. They do this by physically limiting the flow of information. A digital diode physically assures that information can only flow in one direction with the side effect that reliable transmission requires redundancy as it does in a broadcast media, because not even protocol confirmations can be allowed to pass. Lower surety diodes exist as well as similar mechanisms with small covert channels. The ACAT guard and similar technologies are used to allow outward flow of information from more classified to less classified areas by passing it through a human and automated guard station that is certified for the purpose. This allows many covert channels as well as leaking classified information in steganographic or other coded forms.

- **Firewalls and similar permeable barriers** are used to limit the effects of issues on one side of the barrier from impacting other sides of the barrier, while still allowing select information to pass. Modern firewall appliances also include content control mechanisms; however, those are covered separately. Firewalls tend to have demilitarized zones (DMZs) and or proxy servers designed so that packet-level and transport-level attack mechanisms cannot pass through the firewall but are stopped by it. They tend to control allowed protocols, ports, addresses, and to a lesser extent, subprotocol elements. They tend to save state information and often perform network address translation so that direct access between separated network segments cannot work without the firewall present, thus reducing the problem of cross connects and eliminating addressing of systems on other sides of the firewall except those that are supposed to be accessed.

2.6.6.3   Content Controls

Content controls consist of three classes of controls: separation mechanisms such as those identified above, transforms, and filters. These controls operate by examining the syntax and markings associated with content and the situation or context that the content is being applied in.

- **Transforms** are used to encrypt, encode, or authenticate the representation of content so that it is meaningless if illicitly examined, of utility for use in legitimate applications, or detectable if modified. Digital rights management software, encryption hardware and software, virtual private networks (VPNs), and digital signatures are the most common transforms. Transforms are also used on markings associated with content to reflect changes associated with functions performed on the content. Transforms are medium surety level mechanisms if properly used.
- **Filters** limit what is allowed to pass, and include such mechanisms as virus detectors, spam detectors, spyware detectors, Trojan horse detectors, and similar, known, bad-content detection mechanisms. They can also be used to prevent unauthorized syntax and data sequences from passing outward. Known content filters are subject to large numbers of false positives and negatives, leading to their low level of surety as protective mechanisms.
- **Markings** are used as part of content control to allow known and readily readable small amounts of content to be associated with larger nonstructured or more easily modified content so that rapid decisions can be made about access and treatment based on the markings without looking at the syntax of the content itself. For example, classification markings are used in trusted systems to track and separate data and determine accessibility. Markings can also be used in many other similar applications.
- **Syntax** checking is used in most low surety mechanisms to examine the content as a way to determine whether it is known to be of some sort or another. The sort detected by the syntax checking is then used to determine whether to pass or hold the information or treat it in some other manner.
- **Situation** checking is used in conjunction with syntax or markings to determine, based on the state of the application, machine, network, or other situational elements, and what to do with the content. Typically, this involves passing the content, altering it, deleting it, auditing the process, or other similar options.

For high surety content control, it is appropriate to use separation mechanisms such as those identified under access control previously mentioned.

2.6.6.4 *Behavior*

Behavioral mechanisms are used to deal with situations that can be detected by external observation, situations in which behavioral limits can be set regardless of the content or its use, or situations in which controlling behaviors facilitates protection. They include detection of change, times of events, rates of events, fail-safe mechanisms, fault tolerant computing techniques, intrusion or anomaly detection and response, human behavior characterization, detection, and analysis, separation of duties, and least privilege.

- **Change detection and prevention:** Read-only media limits change behavior effectively. As an example, bootable CD-ROMs are used to provide high assurance against changes in the operating environment. When combined with read-only floppy disks for configuration, these systems form medium surety firewalls and similar mechanisms with high surety of regaining original state at reboot. Change detection is useful for many purposes, typically for detecting attempts to alter information as is done in the use of cryptographic checksums in transmission or in storage. Program change detection is critical for assuring integrity of software and is used for virus and malware detection in systems where programs don't change except under proper controls.

- **Time and rate controls:** Control over times and rates are typical of behavioral detection mechanisms. For example, detection of a worker accessing systems at unusual hours or prevention of tellers from making bank transactions after the bank is closed are common mechanisms used in limiting or detecting behaviors based on time. Rate controls have to do with how much happens in a period of time. Examples include methods to limit the rate of transfer of data between locations, rate limiting by traffic type or application, limitations on the rate of responses or queries to databases, etc.

- **Fail-safe systems:** Failure modes that can be identified in advance and safe modes for operation during those failures that can be created to work in the presence of those failures are used to create fail-safe systems. For example, firewalls that disallow all traffic when they fail are common and act as fail-safes (for cases where that mode is safe), whereas detection and response systems that fail by allowing all traffic (which is common for active defenses) are safe for different situations. Most high-surety fail-safe mechanisms are based on physics. For example, a fail-safe water release valve may have a maximum flow rate so that even if a computer tries to release more volume than is allowed, the fail-safe mechanism prevents it by physical limitation. Programmable logic controllers are commonly used in manufacturing processes to provide fail-safes, and similar methods are used in many critical infrastructures.

- **Fault-tolerant computing:** Fault-tolerant computing is designed to be able to detect faults and tolerate them by responding in ways that cover the fault. For example, triple modular redundancy is used in cases where any single failure must be tolerated. Similarly, coding schemes provide for single-error correction and double-error detection in memory for higher integrity computers, in transmission schemes to recover from noise, and in the detection of behavioral patterns that are out of normal behaviors for applications.

- **Intrusion or anomaly detection and response systems:** Detection of most classes of attacks is undecidable, whereas automated response is problematic for all but the simplest situations. Intrusion detection systems detect known intrusion sequences, whereas anomaly detection systems detect changes in behavior that are outside of the normal changes associated with the operation of the system under examination. Response systems can involve anything from logging and notification to automated severing of access. The problem with automated response is that it can be used for reflexive control or similar disruptive effects unless detection is very precise and accurate. The goal should be to detect event sequences with potentially serious negative consequences in time to respond so as to mitigate consequences to within tolerable limits.

- **Human behavior detection and analysis:** Detection and analysis of human behaviors and behavioral changes when using computers is also within the realm of modern technology. Various characteristics of individuals can be identified, characterized, mapped to individuals, and used to detect various conditions. Examples include detection of different people by keystroke and error patterns, detection of command selection and usage in command-based computer use, and detection of normal patters such as reading email periodically at intervals during the day versus reading it as it arrives. As is the case for intrusion detection, the goal is to detect event sequences with potentially serious negative consequences in time to respond so as to mitigate consequences to within tolerable limits.

- **Separation of duties:** Many behaviors are undesired to the point where they have to be independently verified. A good example is the separation of submission of a transaction from commitment to that transaction, the so-called submit–commit cycle. Another good example is the need for multiple approvals before performing a dangerous operation, such as the requirement that two independent operators turn keys simultaneously in order to launch a missile. Separation of duties is a behavioral constraint mechanism that prevents illicit behaviors from happening, even when an authorized insider decides to undertake an inappropriate action of significant magnitude.

- **Least privilege:** The principle of least privilege is based on the notion that users, processes, and other subjects should not have privileges they don't need. As a behavioral control mechanism, least privilege limits behaviors to those that are required in order to carry out the functions that provide the desired utility. For example, process lineage has been used to limit which programs can be run from where, so that users can carry out all of their normal activities, but any attempt to run a program different from the normal user process behavior is blocked or changed to an appropriate alternative. Similarly, many server programs give up privileges after startup to force any attacker attempting to exploit a flaw to be limited in the privileges they can gain as a result.

Behavioral mechanisms come in different surety levels depending on the specifics of the mechanisms used. There are many behavioral detection and response technologies to choose from, but care must be taken because this particular class of technologies provides widely varying surety, depending on the specifics of the implementation and the behaviors being allowed or blocked.

2.7 Roll-Up of the Drill-Down

Content and its business utility drive the need for protection, but protection can also drive out some of the business utility. The goal of effective protection is to assure business utility by efficiently and effectively protecting that utility in order to facilitate proper business operations. This is done by the protective mechanisms put in place and the processes that control them.

Protective mechanisms contact the content and the mechanisms that use that content as well as the threats to that content and its utility. These mechanisms include perception-based, structure-based, content-based, and behavior-based mechanisms that are controlled by protection processes.

Protection processes include the work flow mechanisms; attack and defense processes which deter, prevent, detect, react, and adapt to threats; and data state controls that deal with information at rest, in motion, and in use differently, and they interact with elements of the technical security architecture.

The technical security architecture deals with issues of life cycles, particularly in the area of systems and data life cycles, and context in terms of time, location, purpose, behavior, identity, and method of use within the context of the overall control architecture.

The control architecture typically consists of requirements for integrity, availability, confidentiality, use control, and accountability that are fulfilled by sets of access controls, functional units, perimeters, access methods, and change controls. Change controls limit what changes can be made based on the surety requirements of the content and its utility, which in turn is driven by the risks associated with that content and utility. Access methods provide the means by which identified subjects are authenticated and authorized to use content and gain its utility. Perimeters form the separation mechanisms between zones that allow grouping of surety requirements and risks into pools of manageable size and similar control requirements. Functional units are the mechanisms that implement the architectural concepts and the business utility of the content. Access control schema associate clearance requirements of subjects with classifications of content and its utility in conjunction with risk aggregation requirements and perimeters and access methods to model the control of access. Protection objectives stem from the business needs and surety levels associated with risk management.

In execution, organizations have to do everything that is done to operate their systems and protect their content and its utility. This involves management, policies, standards, procedures, documentation, auditing, testing, technologies, personnel, incident handling, legal, physical security, knowledge, awareness, and organizational aspects and processes. These processes are influenced by the CISO, and the results of these influences are measured and sensed by the CISO using a combination of technical and nontechnical means within the overall governance architecture of the enterprise in order for the CISO to carry out his duties. These processes are also critical parts of the life cycles of people and businesses within the enterprise and these aspects must be managed as well.

The CISO is guided by and contributes to the risk management process that turns duty to protect into what to protect and how well, through the evaluation of risks and matching of surety to risks. Oversight defines these duties to protect by combining legal and regulatory requirements with contractual requirements and self-imposed requirements. This is ultimately driven by business requirements that support the people and things, and the business processes that cause the business to operate.

Chapter 3

Summary and Conclusions

This guidebook is intended to give an overall guide to the CISO function. It provides a broad introduction to the job and its elements, and a drill-down into many of the issues that the CISO faces. It provides guidance as to how CISOs and enterprises operate today and gives specific examples of how governance works and its limitations.

The guidebook starts with the structure of information protection within an enterprise and gives an outline of what a comprehensive information protection program looks like. This includes how the business works, how oversight is done and by whom, how risk management operates and where it fits in, how the CISO function fits into business structures, control architecture, and how it drives technical security architecture, protection processes, and protective measures. It goes on to characterize the CISO's position with respect to others in management, budgets, and how the protection process is funded, how the appeals and enforcement process lead to an overall control system. Finally, it reviews how long it takes to make the sorts of changes associated with the CISO function in an enterprise.

A drill-down follows to detail the next layer of information required for the CISO. This includes specifics of the different aspects of the protection program put into the context of the different people that have responsibilities, how they work together, what has to be done, and how it gets done. It provides details of many aspects of the protection program to the level required for effective measurement of the protection program at the CISO level.

While there is a reasonable attempt to be comprehensive, coverage may be lacking in specific areas of interest. We hope to update this coverage to meet the changing times but can only do this with your help. As a reader of this work, it is our hope as its authors that you will provide feedback so we can improve our presentation and update our content based on your comments. We look forward to your feedback and appreciate your time and effort in giving it to us.

Index

A

Access control, 96
  application-level, 114
  architecture, 118, 123
  decisions, 123
  identity management infrastructure for, 99
  location and, 128
  mechanisms, 158, 174
Access process architecture, 124–126
  authentication, 125
  identification, 124–125
Accountability, 12, 116–118
  costs, 33
  low-surety systems, 56
Accreditation, 12
Adaptation, 165–167
Anomaly detection, 123, 124, 176, 177
  goal, 161
  system calibration, 162
Appeals, 20, 34
Architecture
  access process, 124–126
  change control, 126
  logical perimeter, 122–124
  technical security, 127–128
Assessment, 12
Audit(s), 26, 79, 97
  cost, 33
Authentication, 158
Authorization, 158
Awareness, 12, 27, 108–110
  attacker, 156
  badging and carding, 109
  computer-based, 109
  cost, 33
  costs, 17, 32, 33
  games, 109

  group, 25, 29, 80, 109
  lectures, 109
  levels, 101
  life cycles and, 136
  of sanction policies and consequences, 157
  posters and banners, 109
  programs, 5, 16, 40, 71, 75, 79
    award, 109, 110
    CISO, 108–109
    covert, 110
    department meetings, 108
    document review in, 108
    initial briefings in, 108
    reward, 109
    social, 110
  requirements, 79
  review board, 29
  specialist, 27
  stand-downs, 110
  teams, 41
  video-based, 109

B

Background checks, 40, 101, 116, 124, 135
Backups, 99, 145, 146, 149, 171–172
  file server, 150–151
  long-term, 151
  RAID, 149–150
  removable media, 150
  restoration from, 145–146
  time spent in, 17
  transaction-based remote, 151
Boyd cycle, 103, 167. *See also* OODA loop
Business
  bankruptcy, 134
  characteristics, 44–46

T - #0267 - 101024 - C0 - 254/178/12 [14] - CB - 9780849384356 - Gloss Lamination